BRIGHT IDEAS

Science

Compiled by Jill Bennett and Roger Smith

Published by Scholastic Ltd,
Villiers House, Clarendon Avenue,
Leamington Spa,
Warwickshire, CV32 5PR

© 1984 Scholastic Ltd

12 13 14 15 16   67890

Ideas drawn from Scholastic magazines.

Compiled by Jill Bennett and Roger Smith
Edited by Philip Steele
Illustrations by Ken Stott

Printed in England by
Clays Ltd, St Ives plc

ISBN 0 590 70833 3

Front cover: Water-lily and hover-flies, Oxford Scientific Films. Back cover: Red cabbage – cross-section, Oxford Scientific Films.

CONTENTS

INTRODUCTION

Primary science as we see it is essentially *practical*. Children have a questioning attitude to their environment. This natural curiosity should be the springboard to a practical investigation of the child's world.

Children do not necessarily work in a logical way, as any teacher knows. Nevertheless, even at this level, scientific activity should comprise three phases: the collection of evidence, the investigation of evidence, and the attempt to explain evidence. Each of these phases encourages the development of intellectual skills.

COLLECTING EVIDENCE

The key to this first stage is observation – making use of *all* the child's senses. Young children have an eye for detail and a love of questions. With a little help this can be structured and extended. Remember that children do not put subjects into little boxes – history, science and so on. Their activities can relate to any aspect of their environment.

Detailed observation can be followed by ordering, comparing, counting, measuring, describing and reporting. Crucial skills are the interpretation and following of a sequence of instructions. Recording evidence and reporting it uses essential language skills, and this can be enhanced by the regular use of tape recorders, simple cameras, displays, rubbings, plaster casts, graphs, etc. It is far more important that this is the children's own work than that an immaculate display should be mounted by the teacher.

INVESTIGATING EVIDENCE

The skills involved in this stage of the scientific process include the classifying of evidence and the search for patterns. Perhaps the hardest thing – for the non-specialist teacher as well as for the child – is how to plan the investigation in a scientific way. It is important that the children should recognize when a test is fair, and plan it accordingly.

The older or more advanced children will need to consider the different factors which will affect the test – scientists call this 'isolating variables'. Suppose that you are investigating a pendulum. What are the factors affecting its operation? The length of the string, the weight of the bob, and whether the bob is released or pushed, are all variables. But which will speed up or slow down the swing? To make the test fair, each factor must be varied in turn, leaving the other two variables the same. It should soon become clear that it is only the length of the string which affects the swing time.

By making graphs, the child should be encouraged to predict the outcome of the investigations.

EXPLAINING EVIDENCE

The crucial skill in the final phase of the scientific process is sound reasoning. The child can begin to relate cause and effect, and distinguish between observation and inference. Just as important is the ability to think imaginatively. The result of the investigation, once ascertained, should spark off further questions and enquiries.

The final part of the process should involve the children being encouraged to make some kind of a record of the whole investigation – words, pictures, displays, or whatever. If you do not think it is worth recording, was it worth doing in the first place?

The aim of this process should not be to transmit a body of knowledge to the child – although knowledge will, of course, be acquired – but to instil an ability to find things out, and to tackle problems effectively.

If all the theory sounds very serious, do not be deterred. Teaching science is fun, and if the teacher finds it enjoyable, so will the children.

SCIENCE IN THE CURRICULUM

Science activities will encourage children to develop enquiring minds, to enjoy practical activities and to persevere with problems. It will also develop manipulative skills in the use of equipment. Studies related to their own bodies should aim to give children self-confidence and a positive self-image, whilst studies related to natural history should extend children's interest and concern to animals, plants and the environment in general.

SCIENCE IN THE CLASSROOM

Teaching style is very much a personal matter. The way one goes about things depends a great deal on the individual and his or her children. Some teachers are happy with a lot less structure than others. Flexibility is, however, very important when it comes to science, as is the ability to stand back and observe the children, to listen to what they have to say. One must have sensitivity, so that their natural curiosity and investigative instincts are not stifled by ideas imposed on them.

Whatever style is adopted, organization is of paramount importance. It is the key to taking advantage of spontaneous interest, to seizing that 'teachable' opportunity. Accessibility of equipment is vital. It is no good spending valuable time and energy scurrying around trying to find bits and pieces during teaching time. Ideally, all that the children are likely to need should be readily available to them in the classroom or resource area.

We suggest that you accumulate a bank of useful items. Non-living materials might include string of various kinds, rubber bands, elastic, papers, stones, woods, fabrics, springs, plastics, metals, cork, chicken wire, Vaseline, foodstuffs, kitchen chemicals such as baking powder and salt, sponge, foam rubber, aluminium foil, Plasticine, plaster of Paris, paints, oil (cooking, olive, machine), candlewax and sawdust. Live items might include guinea-pigs, gerbils, mice, hamsters, goldfish, tortoises, wild birds, earthworms, spiders, wood-lice, ants, snails, ladybirds, algae, moulds, yeast, plants (decorative, useful and food), including seeds, bulbs, corms and trees, bones, shells and teeth. Equipment to hand should include clipboards, measuring and recording equipment.

The way of approaching science and introducing topics depends on the particular conditions, class size, etc. With the youngest children especially, spontaneous interest often arises from activity in the classroom, from items brought in by children, or from an event during the day. The teacher must ask questions to seek out matters of scientific interest associated with the object or implicit in the activity. Some teachers might care to use a story or a poem as a starting point. Others may choose to approach science through a general topic such as 'food' or 'transport'. Some may select a more overtly scientific topic, such as 'air'. Others may care to start with a specific scientific activity, and develop it over a number of sessions, with small groups of children.

Whilst some activities may benefit from a whole-class approach, more often than not it is best to work in small groups, which can talk to each other and report back to the whole class. Those teachers with little or no experience of classroom science may prefer to begin with one group working on a science activity whilst the rest are engaged in other areas of the curriculum. The number of science groups can be increased as confidence grows. The important thing is to *start*. From small and simple beginnings science can develop steadily. Always remember: encourage the children to think, to ask questions, to do and to care.

In science, language is often used in a precise way. Special words are used in relation to processes, or specific meanings are given to common words in everyday use, such as power or energy. Try to use the correct scientific terms from the start, even with the youngest children.

And one final plea: *never* underestimate your children!

HOW TO USE THIS BOOK

Each topic in this book is designed for use in the ordinary classroom, with very little, if any, use of specialized equipment. Although the topics are of different lengths, each one contains a range of ideas and activities for children of the primary age range.

A guide is given to the appropriate age for the activity in question, but age need not necessarily determine the level of activity in which children become involved. Experience of scientific and investigative activity is the most important consideration. Fourth-year juniors with little experience will make excellent use of material perhaps designed for experienced infants.

Each project includes a list of materials that the teacher or the children will need to assemble before or during the course of the activity. Make sure that you use all available resources to support your teaching: TV and radio programmes, microcomputers, work-cards, broadcast pamphlets, teachers' source books and children's topic books. Where testing charts are mentioned in the list of requirements, you will find the relevant chart for each activity in the 'Charts to copy' section at the back of the book. These charts may be copied and distributed for use in school only. You may find it useful to have a supply of clipboards for the children to use with their charts. Throughout the book you will notice a danger symbol (a cross inside a circle) next to any diagrams where extra care must be taken to ensure the children's safety.

Roger Smith
Jill Bennett

5

BRIDGE
THAT GAP

Shapes and strengths

Age range
Five to seven.

Group size
Small group.

What you need
Geo-strips,
straws,
sticky tape,
Plasticine,
pipe-cleaners.

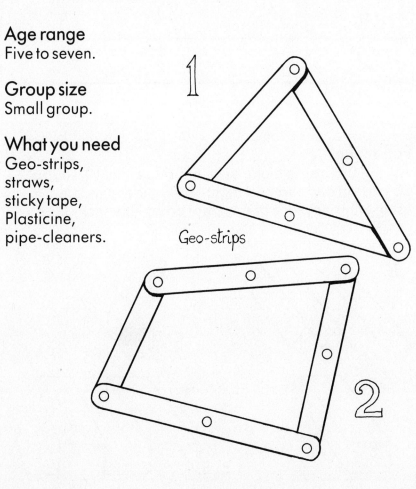

Geo-strips

What to do
Get the children talking about shapes. What shapes can they make by fastening together pieces of Geo-strip? They can alter the shapes of triangles and quadrilaterals by pushing them from side to side.

Follow-up 1
Which is firmer, shape 1 or shape 2? Why do you think that is? How can other strips be added to make the structures firmer?

Recording
The children might draw round two examples of the shapes they have made — one that is firm, and one that can be altered by pushing.

Follow-up 2
Older children can try to make a cube using plastic drinking straws. Leave the method of fixing the corners to the children: they may use sticky tape, Plasticine, pipe-cleaners, etc. What happens to the cube when you hold the base and push the top over? How can you make it stronger?

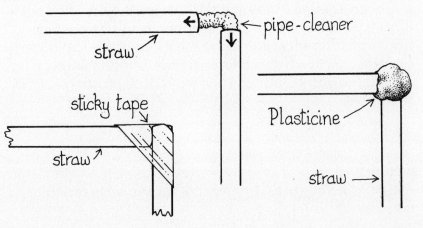

pipe-cleaner

straw

sticky tape

straw

Plasticine

straw

Folding paper

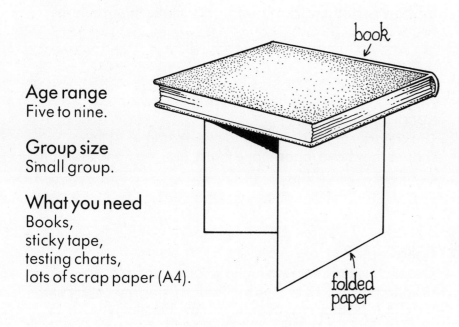

book

folded paper

Age range
Five to nine.

Group size
Small group.

What you need
Books,
sticky tape,
testing charts,
lots of scrap paper (A4).

What to do
Can any of the children manage to balance a piece of paper on its edge? They can't! However, they will find out that it's possible if they fold the paper in half. Take some books of different weights and see if they can be balanced on folded paper. If the children try out different ways of folding the paper, they will find ways of supporting quite a few books.

Recording
The children can use a testing chart as shown to record their results.

shape	number of books
1	3
2	1

Follow-up
Ask the children to make a paper bridge that will span a 20-cm gap and carry a weight of 100 g in the middle, using only one piece of A4 paper and a little sticky tape.

1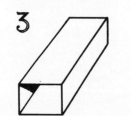

2

3

4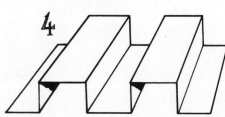

They may fold the paper into all kinds of shapes. Can the children suggest a test to discover how much weight the different bridges will hold? Again, they should record their results on a testing chart.

Girders

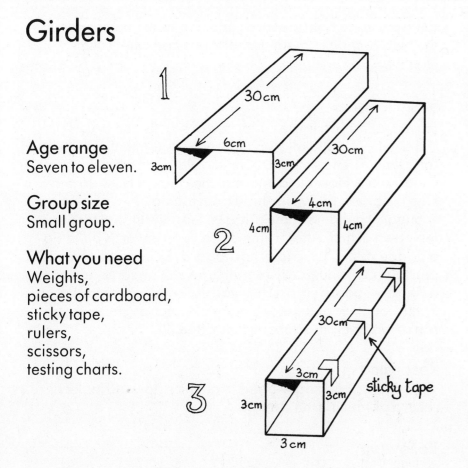

Age range
Seven to eleven.

Group size
Small group.

What you need
Weights,
pieces of cardboard,
sticky tape,
rulers,
scissors,
testing charts.

What to do
The challenge of making a bridge from paper has now been met. The skills used can be extended so that children begin to make bridges from cardboard girders of different sizes. They can make three kinds of girder from three pieces of cardboard measuring 12 × 30 cm. Will each kind of girder support the same weight?

Recording
The children can test the girder bridges they have made and record the results on charts. What sort of questions should be asked at this point? Which girder is strongest? Why? Does it make any difference if the weights are put on in different places? Does doubling the thickness of card make the bridge twice as strong? Will two girders side by side hold twice as much weight? Is there any difference if the girders are fixed together in some way?

Bricks and arches

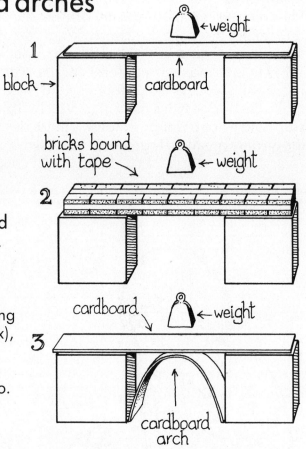

1

block → | ← cardboard | ← weight

bricks bound with tape →

2 ← weight

3

cardboard | ← weight

cardboard arch

Age range
Five to seven.

Group size
Small group.

What you need
Wooden bricks,
plastic bricks,
Lego,
wood off-cuts,
large interlocking
bricks (eg Unifix),
cardboard,
sticky tape,
plastic Meccano.

Young children playing with bricks and blocks are involving themselves with the basic principles of structures. When a tower topples because a brick has not been put in the right place, a child begins to find out about the construction of buildings, bridges and other such structures.

What to do
Have available a large collection of blocks and bricks of different kinds and allow children to experiment with them for a time. Then ask them to build a wall with a hole or a window in it. How big a hole can they make? How do they stop the bricks above the hole from falling?

Suggest building some bridges. Let the children try on their own at first. After a time direct them towards building a bridge with a flat strip of cardboard (1). Then ask them to join together a number of small bricks to the same length as the cardboard strip. (They can use small cubes taped tightly together or interlocking bricks such as Unifix.) Make this brick structure into a bridge (2).

Recording
The children can add weights to each bridge and make a record of which is the stronger.

Follow-up
Ask the children if they have seen a bridge held up from underneath. What held it up? By making a curved arch from card and fitting it under the first bridge they made, the children will see how an arch can be used to strengthen a structure (3).

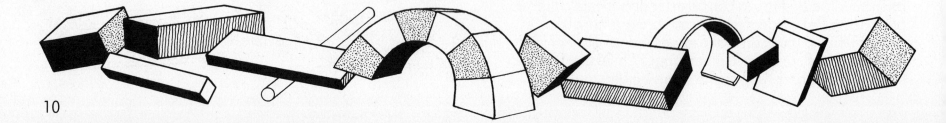

Bridges and weights

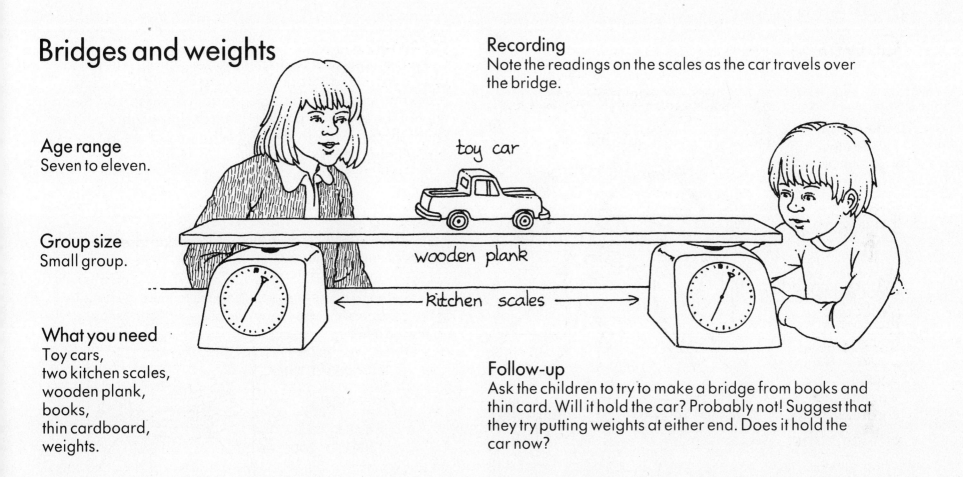

Age range
Seven to eleven.

Group size
Small group.

What you need
Toy cars,
two kitchen scales,
wooden plank,
books,
thin cardboard,
weights.

What to do
Start the children talking about bridges and the sort of loads they have to carry. If a bridge is made from two kitchen scales with the pans removed and a length of wood, children can investigate what happens when a toy car is pushed across. Make sure that both scales are set to zero once the wood is in place.

Recording
Note the readings on the scales as the car travels over the bridge.

Follow-up
Ask the children to try to make a bridge from books and thin card. Will it hold the car? Probably not! Suggest that they try putting weights at either end. Does it hold the car now?

Recording
Ask them to find out the minimum weight needed at each end in order to make the bridge take the car's weight. What about two cars? How much extra weight is needed at each end? Record the results.

11

Curves

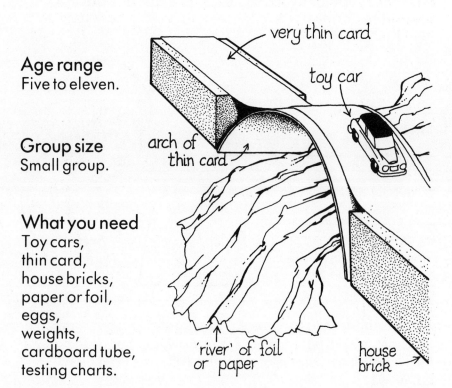

very thin card

toy car

arch of thin card

'river' of foil or paper

house brick

Age range
Five to eleven.

Group size
Small group.

What you need
Toy cars,
thin card,
house bricks,
paper or foil,
eggs,
weights,
cardboard tube,
testing charts.

What to do
Is there a hump-backed bridge over a canal or a railway line near the school? What does driving over it feel like? Why is it constructed in this way? Ask the children to try to make an arched bridge that will hold the weight of a toy car, using only very thin card. It is probably best to use two house bricks as end supports.

Follow-up
Curved shapes such as arches are very strong. They are often used over doors and windows; to build tunnels; for pipes and straws. In nature, eggs gain strength from their curved shape, which protects them during incubation. The children might care to investigate how much weight an egg will support. It's quite a lot!

Recording
Test different weights as in the diagram and record the results on testing charts.

The Egg Test

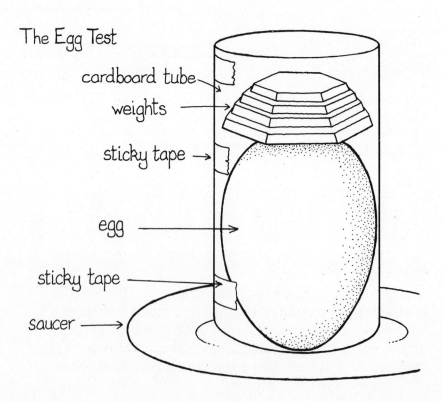

cardboard tube

weights

sticky tape

egg

sticky tape

saucer

Suspension

Age range
Seven to eleven.

Group size
Small group or whole class.

What you need
Card,
cotton thread,
basketry cane,
house bricks,
weights,
testing charts.

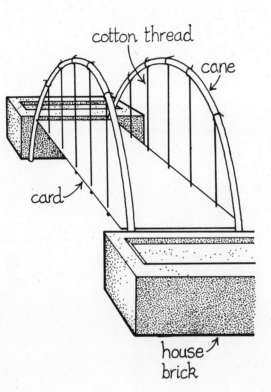

cotton thread

cane

card

house brick

What to do
Show the children pictures of suspension bridges. Ask them to try to make one from cotton, card and cane. The cane must be held up by taut cotton, not by resting on the bricks. Ask the children why people use this method for building bridges. What are the disadvantages of piles and arches?

Recording
Ask the children to suggest how they would test how much weight the bridge can hold. They can record the results of their findings.

Round and about

Age range
Seven to eleven.

Group size
Small group or whole class.

What you need
Clipboards,
pencils and paper.

What to do
The children make a survey of bridges in the neighbourhood, sketching or photographing them. Mention five kinds of bridge: single beam, girder/truss, arch, suspension, cantilever. Explain how they work. Can they find pictures of each kind?

Follow-up
The children will soon begin to recognize shapes which provide strong support. Ask them to find 20 places around school where arches and triangles are used to take stress and strain – metal-legged chairs, windows and doors, roof and temporary building supports, etc.

B
B
BOUNCE
A BALL

Starter

Age range
Five to eleven.

Group size
Small group or
whole class.

What you need
Paper,
pens,
all kinds of balls.

What to do
Make a collection of balls: football, rugby, cricket,
volley-ball, rounders, tennis, golf, squash, beach-balls,
rubber balls, sponge balls. Invite the children to add
further examples. These can include any spherical objects
such as marbles, beads, ball-bearings, gob-stoppers and
so on. Let them play with them.

Then ask the children to sort the balls into groups.
Categories could include: soft/hard, rough/smooth,
bouncy/not bouncy, solid/hollow. The different sets can
be drawn and labels attached to the balls – a few words
describing each example. Do any of the balls fit into more
than one group?

Measuring bounce

Age range
Five to nine.

Group size
Small groups.

What you need
Selection of balls,
clipboards,
paper,
pens,
testing charts,
metre rules,
timers.

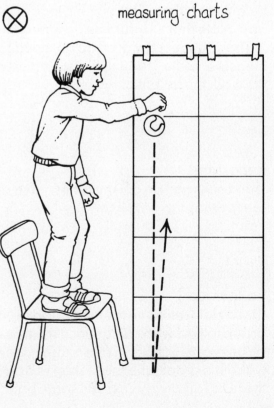

measuring charts

15

What to do

Let each member of the group take a ball at random and try to bounce it. Some will have difficulty controlling the bounce. Use this to start an investigation. What do you think makes a ball bounce? Which balls are the best bouncers? What do we mean by 'best'? Is it the height of the bounce, or the speed, or the ease of bounce? The children must decide what they are testing before starting. Suggest they try bouncing the ball on the carpet. Does this make a difference? Why? What about a hard, polished surface?

When young children are investigating the ball's bounce, you will need to tell them that the same person should act as dropper and release the ball at the same height each time. This eliminates all but one variable – the ball. Note that it should be *dropped* and not *thrown*.

The youngest children do not need to use standard measurements. If you pin large sheets of squared paper to the wall, the height of the bounce can be marked on them.

Recording

The results can be put into order, and displayed for all to see, perhaps in graph form.

Follow-up 1

Once children have found a good ball for bouncing, ask a group to find who can bounce it the best. They could look at the most bounces in one minute; the most bounces without a break; the time taken to do 20 bounces. To make the tests fair always use the same ball.

Recording

Did the best bouncer bounce the ball high or low? Were the bounces high or low for the poorest bouncer? Was the person who bounced the ball fastest bending low or standing straight? Did his or her feet get in the way?

Follow-up 2

Ask the children to investigate how a ball bounces by drawing bounce patterns on sheets of paper . . . these will make an attractive wall display. Questions worth considering are: do all balls bounce in the same way when dropped from a given height (say, one metre)? Do all balls bounce the same number of times? Do any balls return to the same height after the first bounce?

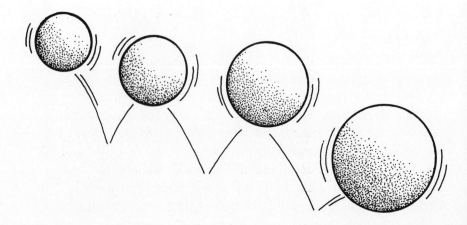

Splat factor

Age range
Seven to eleven.

Group size
Pairs.

What you need
Flour,
Plasticine,
rubber balls,
squared paper,
metre rule,
testing charts.

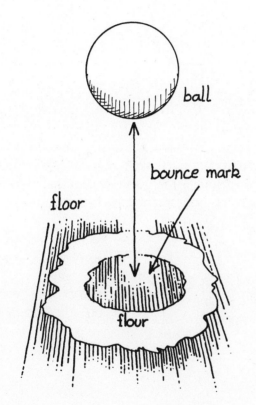

ball

bounce mark

floor

flour

What to do
Children can investigate the elasticity of a soft rubber ball
by spreading flour on the floor and dropping the ball on to
it. Is the mark in the flour larger, smaller or the same size
as the mark made by just touching the flour with the ball?
How much difference is there?

Recording
Repeat the test for several different balls. The children
should compare the results and record them. Remember, if
the test is to be fair, the balls must be dropped from the
same height each time.

Follow-up
When a Plasticine ball is dropped from a height of two
metres, it 'splats' on the floor. The children might
investigate how much the height of the drop affects the
'splat' area. Use squared paper to measure the area.
Keep the tests as fair as possible. Try to explain
the findings.

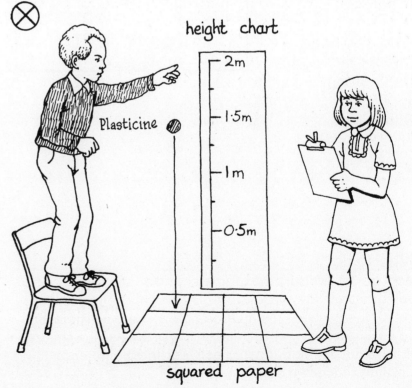

height chart

Plasticine

2m

1·5m

1m

0·5m

squared paper

17

Measuring balls

Age range
Seven to eleven.

Group size
Pairs or small group.

What you need
Wooden blocks or
bricks, string,
displacement container,
balls,
squared paper,
pencils.

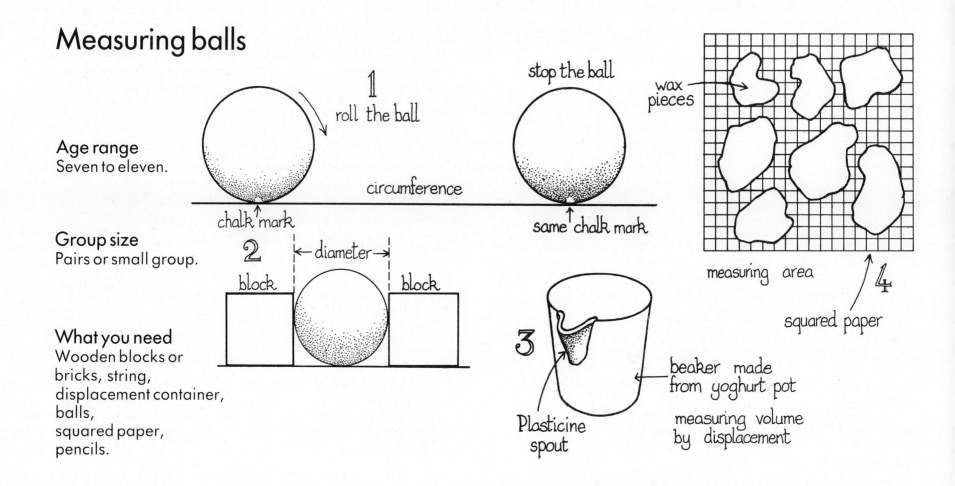

What to do
How do we measure the diameter and circumference of a
ball as accurately as possible? Let the children try to find
out for themselves. The methods shown here will help, but
do not show them to the children too soon. Ask the children
to try to find the relationship between the diameter and
circumference of a ball.

Follow-up
You may have already done some work on volume
displacement with the older children. They could try to find
the volume of a ball by measuring the amount of water
displaced by it. They might try to measure the surface area
of a ball as well. This may be done by covering a ball in hot
wax (**take care!**). When it is cold the wax can be peeled off
and measured on squared paper.

Superstars

Age range
Seven to eleven.

Group size
Whole class.

What you need
Balls and PE equipment,
testing charts,
timers,
pencils.

Children are usually very interested in ball skills. A great deal of science can be learned from a ball skills 'superstars' competition.

What to do
Arrange a competition in the different ball skills – catching, throwing, dribbling, shooting, kicking, bouncing, etc. All the activities must be fair: counting, timing, measuring and observation must be carried out by the children.

Recording
Results must be recorded. Try to display all the findings and ask the children to explain them. They should think about the methods, size, experience, etc, of those taking part.

Roller-coasters

Age range
Five to eleven.

Group size
Pairs or small groups.

What you need
Books,
plank,
ball,
marbles,
cardboard,
tape-measure,
testing charts,
clipboards,
pencils.

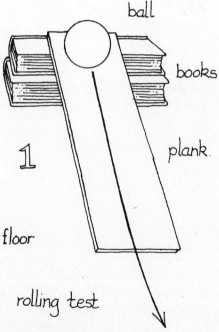

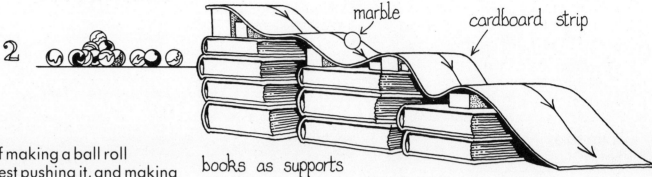

2

marble

cardboard strip

books as supports

What to do
Discuss with the children ways of making a ball roll further. They will probably suggest pushing it, and making a slope for it to roll down. Let them try rolling it down a plank (1). How far does it roll down the plank? Or along the floor? Or both together? Is there a relationship between the height of the slope and the distance the ball rolls? Does doubling the height double the distance rolled? Does the surface on which the ball rolls alter the distance it travels?

Recording
Note the results on charts and display them as histograms.

Follow-up
The children can make a roller-coaster (2) from card and marbles. How big can the highest bump be if the marble is released from a height of one metre? Does it make a difference if the highest bump is at the end or near the start?

Inflatables

Age range
Five to eleven.

Group size
Small groups.

What you need
Inflatable ball or leather football and ball pump, metre rule, testing chart, squared paper, pencils and pens.

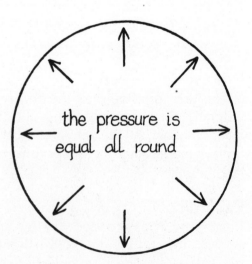

the pressure is equal all round

What to do

The children find out about the bounce of an inflatable ball. An old-fashioned leather football is ideal, but if this is hard to come by, any inflatable ball will do. Start by looking at a deflated ball. Can the children explain how and why it becomes hard? Is it as equally hard all over when it is blown up?

The children can find out whether the ball bounces highest when it is blown up as hard as possible. Start with a deflated ball and measure the bounce at regular intervals (so many puffs or pumps). Drop the ball from the same height each time.

Recording

Record the results and show them on a bar graph. Can the children explain their findings?

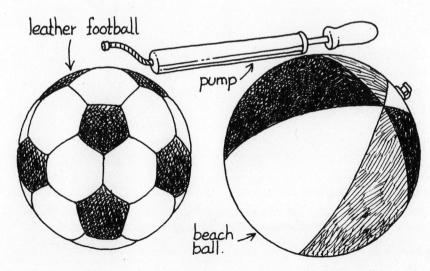

leather football

pump

beach ball.

Falling balls

Age range
Seven to eleven.

Group size
Pairs.

What you need
Selection of balls,
paper,
clipboards,
testing charts,
pencils,
step-ladder or chairs.

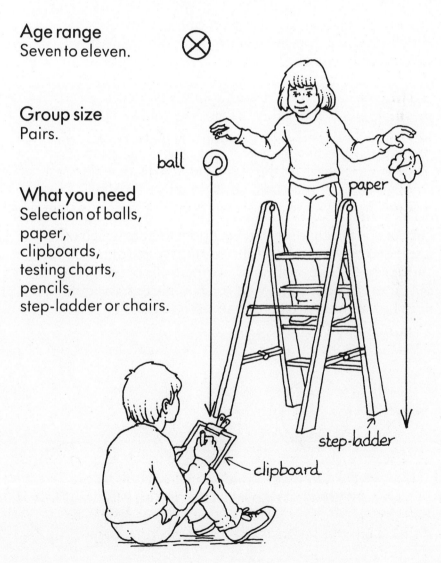

ball

paper

step-ladder

clipboard

What to do

The children can try dropping a ball from a given height and watching it fall. A chair or table should do for heights of up to two metres, but greater heights may demand the use of a step-ladder or a staircase: **ensure safety at all times!** Compare the fall of the ball with that of a piece of crumpled paper, and then try dropping the two simultaneously from the same height. Which hits the ground first, and why?

Recording

The children should record the results and try to explain their findings.

Follow-up

Encourage the children to investigate factors which affect the speed at which a ball falls. Is it mass, size or the ball's surface area? They will need to drop balls of equal size but different mass – and vice versa. Only one variable must be changed at a time if the test is to be fair.

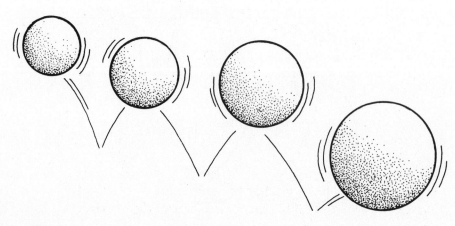

Angles of bounce

Age range
Seven to eleven.

Group size
Pairs.

What you need
Ball,
chalk,
marbles,
large protractor,
clipboard,
testing charts,
tape-measure,
cardboard,
flour,
board.

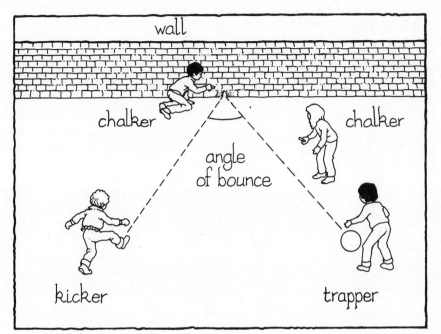

Record variables on testing charts. Is there a pattern to the angles of bounce? What happens if the ball is kicked from different places? Does the wall or ground surface make a difference? Does the force of the kick make a difference?

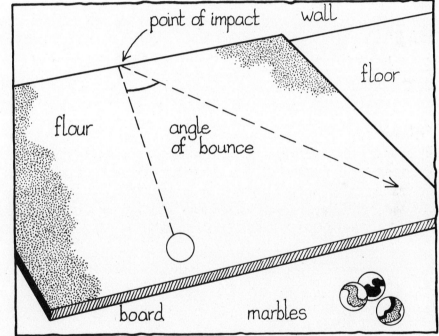

What to do

Get the children talking about the angles of bounce. They can bounce balls vertically or at low angles, catching each others' balls as they bounce. They can draw the bounce patterns and look at the angles made. It is very difficult for children to measure the angles of vertical bounces, but they can try to measure horizontal ones.

With the children working in fours, suggest that one person kicks the ball against a smooth wall, and another traps it on the rebound. A third marks with chalk the impact point on the wall, and a fourth chalks a line between this point, the kicker and the trapper.

Follow-up

Children can also try the test with marbles on a floured surface. The angle of bounce will be traced out in the flour.

23

TIME

Starter

Age range
Five to eleven.

Group size
Small group or whole class.

What you need
Pens,
paper,
picture sequences.

picture sequence cards

What to do
Get the children to talk about how long things take. How long is playtime? Too long? Not long enough? Can the children find out how long it lasts? Which lasts longer – playtime or dinner time? Which takes longer: drinking their milk through a straw or from a glass? How can they find out? Discuss the length of TV programmes.

From talking about the duration of time, move on to clock time. How do they know when to turn on the television for *Dr Who*?

The order in which things happen is an important aspect of understanding time. Present the children with a number of pictures showing a sequence of events: a day at home, a day at school, making a cup of tea, and so on. Can they put them in order? Discuss their efforts: there may be individual differences in routine.

paper or card

picture clock

Follow-up
Ask individuals to make a sequence of 'my day' showing what they do at various times. They might present this in strip form or as a picture clock.

Shadow games

Age range
Five to eleven.

Group size
Pairs or small groups.

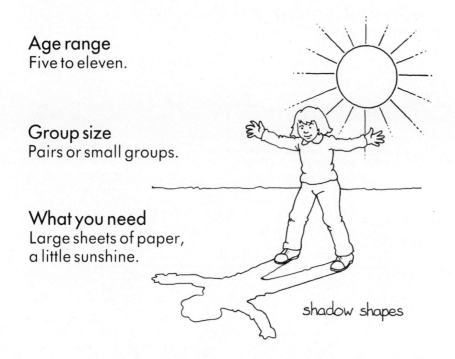

shadow shapes

What you need
Large sheets of paper,
a little sunshine.

What to do
Studying shadows is a good way of learning about time.
On a sunny day play shadow shapes. Ask the children to
make the biggest/smallest/longest shadow they can. Can
they stand so that their shadow falls behind them; in front;
to the side? Can they stand without their shadows moving?

Some children may like to draw round an interesting
shadow shape on a large sheet of paper. Can a group
arrange themselves so that each person's shadow
appears to be standing on the shoulders of another?

Follow-up
Try playing shadow tag with the children. One person is
the chaser and the others in the group run away. If the
chaser touches someone's shadow with their own, then
they call 'freeze!' or 'had!', and that person must stand
still. The last person to be 'had' wins the game.

Moving shadows

playground

marked spot

mark shadows

Age range
Seven to eleven.

Group size
Pairs or small groups.

What you need
Paper,
chalk,
milk bottle,
cricket stump,
pencils,
metre rule,
sunshine.

What to do

A group of children can try making a human shadow map. They mark a spot on the playground, and one child stands on it. The others draw round his or her shadow with chalk and mark the time. The same child returns to that spot at intervals during the day, and the others draw in the new shadow on the ground. Ask what has happened to the shadow. Can they try to explain?

Older children could stand a milk bottle or something similar on the ground to see how the shadow alters as the sun moves round. They should note the time, measure the length and mark the position of the shadow on each occasion. A cricket stump knocked into grass is a good alternative.

Recording

Paper may be fixed to the ground and the bottle placed on it or the stump knocked through it. The positions and times may be drawn in on the paper, which may then be displayed in the classroom.

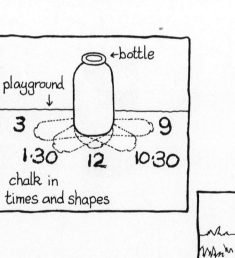

Sundials

Age range
Seven to eleven.

Group size
Pairs or small groups.

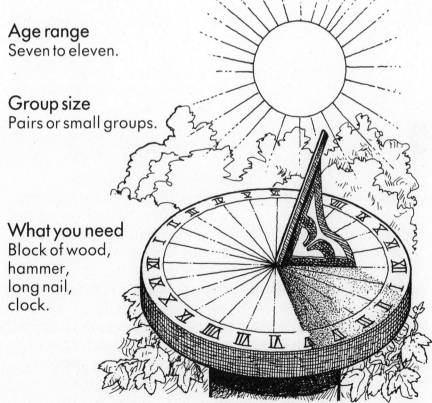

What you need
Block of wood,
hammer,
long nail,
clock.

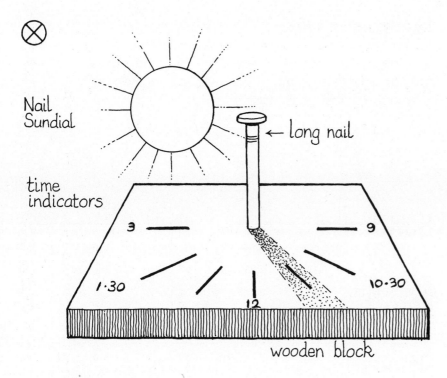

Nail
Sundial

time
indicators

3 — — 9

1·30   10·30

12

long nail

wooden block

What to do

When the children have grasped the concept of how shadows move throughout the day, they can try to make a clock using this principle. A long nail can be hammered into a block of wood to make a simple sundial. Remember that it must be placed in exactly the same place each day – chalk in its outline. On the first day the children should calibrate it using a clock – you may need to help them with this. Suggest that the children try using it to tell the time. Perhaps a group could make a permanent sundial for the school. Can the children see any snags in using a clock like this one? (How will it need to be changed during the year? – BST/GMT. Can it be carried around? Will it work in cloudy weather or indoors?)

Follow-up

Is there a sundial near the school, perhaps in a churchyard, on an old building, or in a park? Sundials can take many forms. Take the children to see how one works.

Timers

Age range
Seven to eleven.

Group size
Small groups.

What you need
Empty washing-up liquid bottles,
glass jars,
stop clock,
pens and markers,
fine sand,
sugar,
salt.

fine sand

bottom
cut off

washing-up
liquid bottle

invert
and rest
on rim
of jar

glass
jar

calibrate
jar

What to do

There are many ways of making short-period timers. Most children are familiar with egg-timers. It is simple enough – and great fun – to make one from a glass jar and an empty washing-up liquid bottle as shown in the diagram. You will have to cut the ends off the bottles before the experiment. Fine sand can be used as the measuring medium.

Recording

Calibrate the bottle to give time readings. How can you alter the time for which it runs? Think about the size of the hole and the quantity of sand. Can you improve the flow of sand? Try other substances, such as salt, sugar, etc. Which works best? The children should record their findings and try to explain them.

Water clocks

Age range
Seven to eleven.

Group size
Small groups.

What you need
Lengths of wood,
water,
plastic cups,
drawing pins.

This very simple water clock will run for only a few minutes, but it is interesting to make and involves a number of different scientific skills.

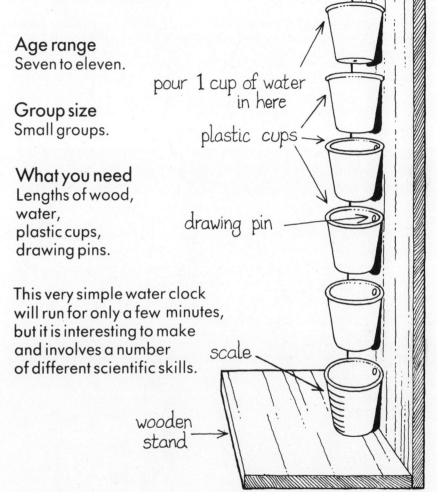

pour 1 cup of water in here

plastic cups

drawing pin

scale

wooden stand

What to do
Make small holes in the bases of all but one cup, then pin them to a length of wood as shown. A scale may be drawn on the bottom, unholed cup. One cupful of water is poured into the top cup, and drips down to the bottom one.

Recording

Does the water always take the same time to reach the bottom? How can you make it run for a longer period? Try and find two ways. What happens when the holes in the cup are made very small? Can this clock be used for telling the time?

Follow-up

Can the children design and make a water clock on their own? The children can find out something about the history of water clocks by referring to the school library.

What you need

Candles,
holders,
markers,
beam balance,
timer,
foil cup.

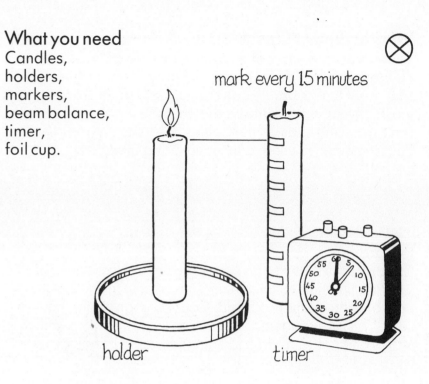

mark every 15 minutes

holder   timer

Candle clocks

Age range
Seven to eleven.

Group size
Small groups.

What to do

Here are some other kinds of clocks made from candles. The first is the most common and very easily made. The children should each have candles of the same size and brand. As one candle burns down, it is timed and the various heights marked off on an unlit candle.

Follow-up

An alternative candle clock may be made using a beam balance. As the candle burns down, the time scale may be marked off accordingly.

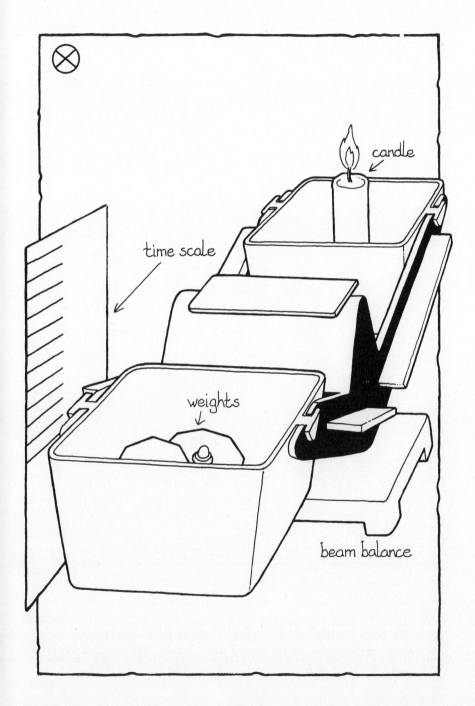

candle

time scale

weights

beam balance

Clock challenge

Age range
Nine to eleven.

Group size
Pairs.

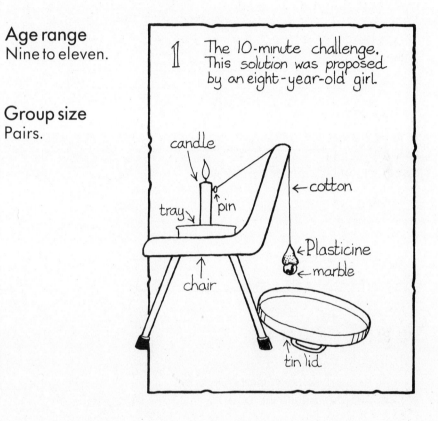

1 The 10-minute challenge.
This solution was proposed
by an eight-year-old girl.

candle

tray

pin

cotton

Plasticine

marble

chair

tin lid

What you need
Items which could be used to make an improvised clock.

What to do
Present a challenge to older children or those who have had experience of designing their own tests: they must design and build a clock that will make a sound at the end of a ten-minute period. See what they can invent without help from you.

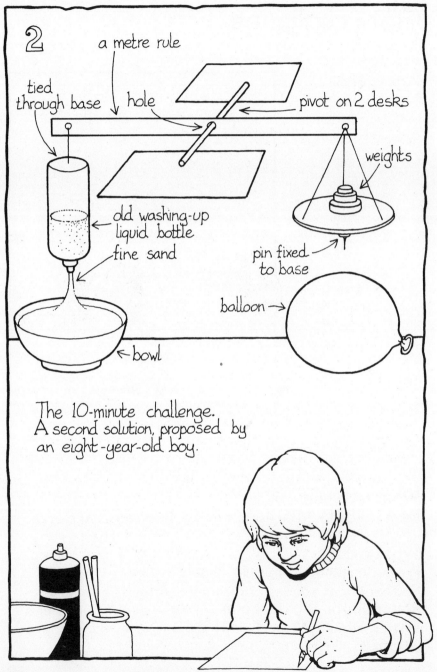

2

a metre rule

tied through base hole pivot on 2 desks

old washing-up liquid bottle
fine sand

weights

pin fixed to base

balloon →

←bowl

The 10-minute challenge.
A second solution, proposed by an eight-year-old boy.

Pendulums

Age range
Seven to eleven.

Group size
Small groups.

What you need
Cotton reels,
beads,
Plasticine,
wooden plank,
drawing pins,
string,
testing chart,
stop clock.

What to do
What is a pendulum? Look at a playground swing and how it works. Let young children play with cotton reels, conkers, threaded beads and Plasticine suspended from string.

Suggest that a group sets up a pendulum made of string and Plasticine, suspended from a plank by a pin. They should swing the pendulum to and fro. What do they notice about the swing? Time 20 swings; how long do they take?

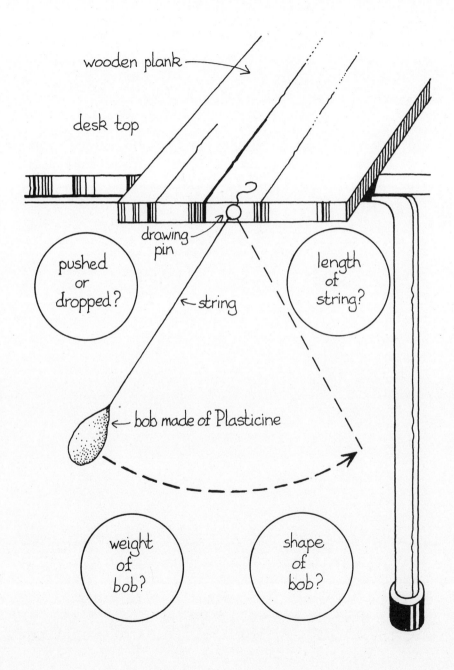

wooden plank

desk top

drawing pin

pushed or dropped?

length of string?

string

bob made of Plasticine

weight of bob?

shape of bob?

'conkers'

Recording
Ask the children to find out what alters the time taken for the pendulum to swing. To make the tests fair they should alter only one variable at a time. Consider these factors: the weight of the bob; the shape of the bob and its air-resistance; the length of the string. The bob should be released gently and evenly: 'push' cannot be easily measured. All the tests should be made three times and the results recorded on charts. Explanatory pictures may be drawn, and graphs produced.

Follow-up
Present the children with a challenge: can they make a pendulum which swings once every second?

33

AIR

Starter

Age range
Five to eleven.

Group size
Whole class.

What you need
Drinking straws,
water,
glass jars.

What to do
As a class, discuss the fact that air is all around us. Can we see it? No. Can we smell it? No. Can we taste it? No. Well, how do we know it's there? Try to lead the discussion towards the *effects* of air: blow on hands, blow paper about, blow bubbles through a straw in water.

On a windy day ask the children to look for things which are moving in or through the air. Look at the trees move. Watch clouds move. Watch leaves and litter blowing about. How are things moving? Quickly or slowly? Up, down or in a straight line (horizontally)? Are they turning or twisting in the air? Give opportunities to observe other things being moved by the air, such as washing on a line, smoke from a chimney or a bonfire. What happens to the children's hair when they go out on a windy day? What happens to their clothes?

Follow-up
The children can list or draw all the things they see which indicate that air is around them. They can start to talk about air moving fast or slowly, and about its force. They might try to devise a scale of air movement based on how much trees sway in the wind.

Pressure 1

Age range
Five to nine.

Group size
Whole class.

What you need
Balloons,
pins,
drinking straws,
old sweet wrappers.

What to do
The children blow up balloons to their full extent, then press the balloons. Do they feel the same all round? Is there any one place on the inflated balloon that is more difficult to press than any other? Why do they think this is so? Make a pin-hole in a deflated balloon. Blow it up carefully. What happens? Listen to the air escaping. Is it coming out at an even rate? Now blow up a balloon and stick a pin in it. What happens? Why do you think this is?

Follow-up
Children can try putting the end of a straw just above a sweet wrapper, and sucking on the straw. What happens? Why? This works on the same principle as a vacuum cleaner: the rush of air pressure pulls up the sweet paper.

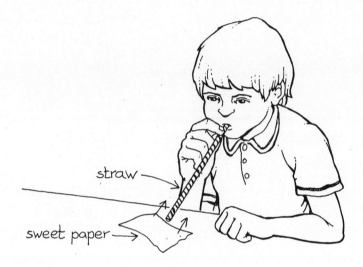

straw

sweet paper

Hot air

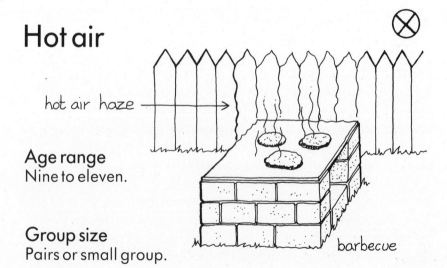

hot air haze

barbecue

Age range
Nine to eleven.

Group size
Pairs or small group.

What you need
Empty washing-up liquid bottle,
balloons,
hot water,
pan.

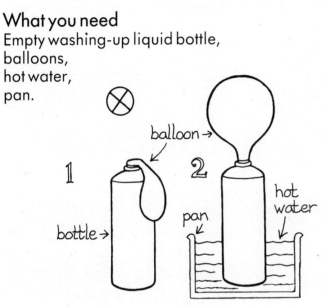

What to do
When you look at the space just above a fire, it appears hazy. The hot air is moving about – rising and disturbing the image you see. Observe this with the children and discuss it. Can they think of any other examples of hot air rising?

Set some of them the task of stretching a balloon over the neck of a small glass bottle or an empty washing-up liquid bottle with the tip removed. Under very close supervision let them pour very hot water around the bottle. What happens to the balloon? Can they explain this?

Recording
Suggest that they draw what they see, and try to explain it.

Breathing

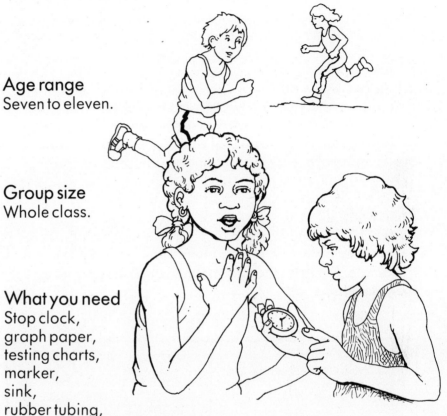

Age range
Seven to eleven.

Group size
Whole class.

What you need
Stop clock,
graph paper,
testing charts,
marker,
sink,
rubber tubing,
storage jar (glass or plastic).

What to do
Ask the children to run around the hall until they are out of breath. Then show them how to measure their breathing rate. One breath means once in and once out. Count the number of breaths in one minute. Who breathes fastest? Who breathes slowest?

Recording
Record the results on testing charts. Make graphs and display them.

Follow-up 1
When they have found out how to record their breathing rate after exercise, ask them to try to find out their *normal* rate. Compare the results. Investigate how quickly their breathing returns to normal after exercise. Do children breathe more quickly than teachers?

Follow-up 2
Older children may care to find out how much air they can breathe out by the methods shown. They can make their own scale. **Don't let them strain themselves: supervise them carefully.**

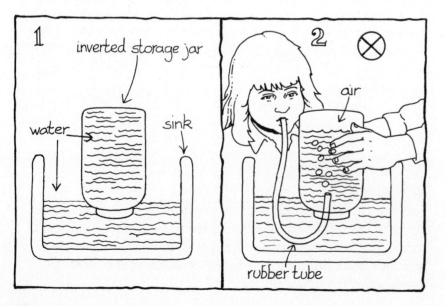

Clouds

Age range
Five to seven.

Group size
Larger group or whole class.

What you need
Card,
paper,
paint and
brushes.

What to do
Get the children to talk about clouds. What are they made of? Why do they move? How do they affect us? Do different clouds produce different types of rain? Look at the shapes of clouds. The children can make a chart of the different clouds they observe. Are all clouds the same colour? Why not? The children can mix paint to match as many cloud colours as possible.

Recording

Children can use charts to record weather over a period (page 121). Can they establish a pattern in the weather? Can they make their own weather forecasts? Why isn't this easy?

Temperature

Age range

Seven to eleven.

Group size

Small groups or whole class.

What you need

A selection of thermometers,
Thermostik,
wire.

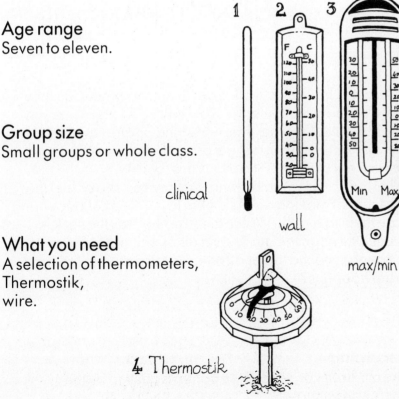

thermometers

1 2 3

clinical

wall

max/min

4 Thermostik

What to do

Get the children talking about heat and cold. Collect a selection of different kinds of thermometer in the classroom. Talk about how they are used. Let the children hold a thermometer bulb in warm hands and watch the temperature rise. Explain how clinical thermometers cover only a very small range of temperature, whereas wall thermometers cover a large range. Suggest that the children measure the temperature inside and outside.

Recording

Children can try taking various temperatures outdoors and recording them on a chart. Ask them if their recordings are accurate. Will a wind make a difference to a recording? Direct sunshine makes *them* feel hotter; do they think the same thing will happen to the thermometer? Recordings can be made at different times of the day: eg 9.30, 12.30, 3 .30. Make a graph of the results. Try to predict the findings.

Follow-up

The children can be set a problem to investigate: is the soil warmer or cooler than the air? A hole can be made in the soil with a stick and a thermometer or Thermostik lowered into it. (Do *not* let them try to dig a hole with the thermometer.) A second thermometer can record the temperature of the air at ground level.

Wind

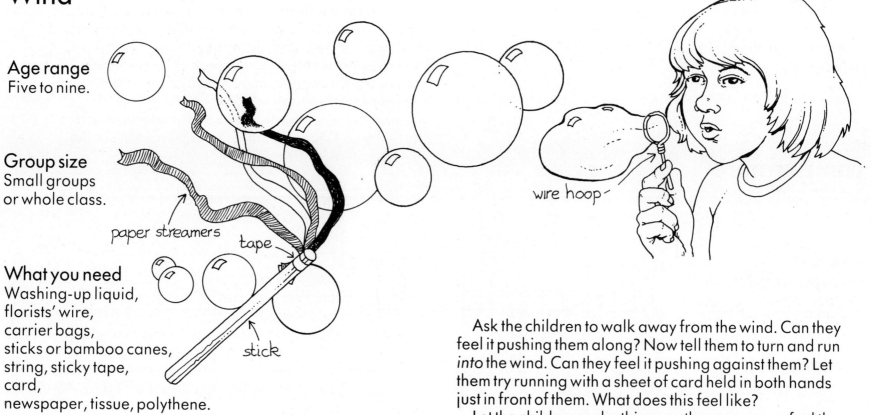

Age range
Five to nine.

Group size
Small groups
or whole class.

paper streamers

tape

stick

wire hoop

What you need
Washing-up liquid,
florists' wire,
carrier bags,
sticks or bamboo canes,
string, sticky tape,
card,
newspaper, tissue, polythene.

What to do
Let the children blow soap bubbles and observe their movement. Blowing hoops are easily made from florists' wire, and washing-up liquid and water mixed in equal proportions make an adequate bubble solution. Try blowing bubbles in different places: outdoors; over a radiator. Can the children see any difference in the way the bubbles move?

Ask the children to walk away from the wind. Can they feel it pushing them along? Now tell them to turn and run *into* the wind. Can they feel it pushing against them? Let them try running with a sheet of card held in both hands just in front of them. What does this feel like?

Let the children make things so they can see or feel the pressure of moving air. Ask them to cut strips of paper and tape them to a stick. Watch the streamers as the stick is passed through the air. Try out other materials. Tie a carrier bag to the top of a cane. Try running into the wind. What happens?

Recording
The children can record the patterns caused by the airflow in pictures.

Measuring wind

Age range
Seven to eleven.

Group size
Small groups or whole class.

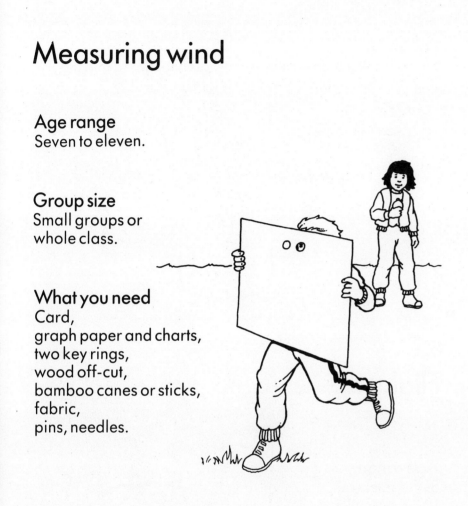

What you need
Card,
graph paper and charts,
two key rings,
wood off-cut,
bamboo canes or sticks,
fabric,
pins, needles.

What to do
Ask the children if they can compete with the wind. They should try running with the wind and against it. Which time is faster? How can they make this a fair test? What distance will they run? Next they should try slowing themselves down with a large sheet of card. Which way should the card be held? Time the run. Now double the card size and repeat. What do they find?

Follow-up
How can you tell that the wind is blowing? Try to make something that will tell you how strong the wind is. Use your own scale. Make instruments that will show from which direction the wind is blowing. The diagrams below may help. If a model doesn't work, suggest rebuilding it and trying again.

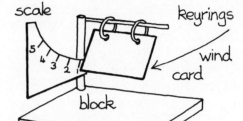

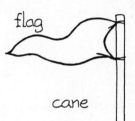

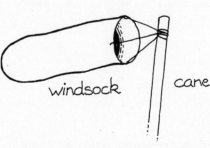

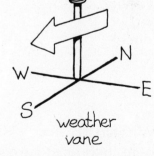

Recording
The children may like to draw plans of their models showing how they work.

Pressure 2

Age range
Seven to eleven.

Group size
Small groups.

What you need
Yoghurt pots,
Plasticine and
Blu-Tack,
needles,
glass jars,
washing-up bowls
and water,
funnel.

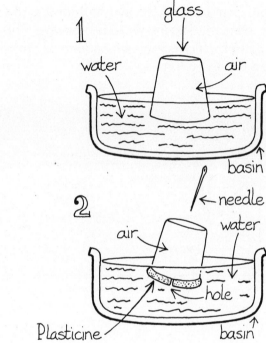

What to do
If the children place a glass upside down in water, the air will not escape. Ask them why. Set a challenge for a small group. Can they make a model that will take exactly one minute to sink? The diagram above shows one way, but remember that you need not show them how straight away! The time taken will vary according to the size of the hole in the Plasticine and the hole in the yoghurt pot.

Follow-up
Set up the test below. Why is the water not going into the jar? Ask the children how they might enable it to.

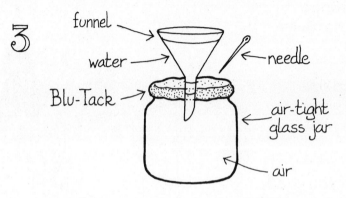

Flight

Age range
Seven to eleven.

Group size
Small groups.

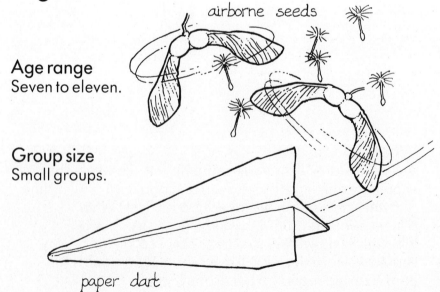

What you need
Paper plates,
shuttlecocks,
small rubber balls,
large plastic balls,
small holey plastic balls,
Plasticine.

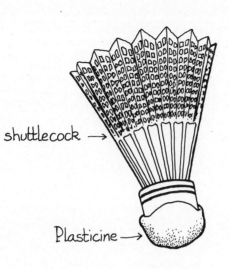

shuttlecock →

Plasticine →

– no flying saucers!). Is it easier to throw a plate than a ball? Does it fly differently?

Throw a shuttlecock in the air. What happens? How does it land? Stick some Plasticine to the base of the shuttlecock. What will happen now? Throw it up into the air and put the children's theories to the test.

paper dart

What to do
Ask children to think about the different ways in which things move through the air. They can draw or list these and then sort them into three sets: things moved by currents of air – seeds with 'parachutes', clouds, kites, feathers, hang-gliders, gliders, litter, etc; things that are thrown into the air with force – balls, darts, paper darts, etc; things which propel themselves through the air – aeroplanes, birds, etc.

What happens to a ball when you throw it straight up in the air? Can you make a ball change direction or curve in mid-air? Children can try throwing different kinds of ball – a large plastic ball, a tennis ball, a holey ball. Which one goes highest? Try throwing up a paper plate (but take care

Follow-up 1
Ask the children to drop a piece of paper from a height of about two metres and watch how it falls. The children should draw the flight path and note which way up the paper lands. Can they design a shape that will drop in a straight line? Does a piece of paper of the same shape always fall in the same way?

Follow-up 2
Paper darts are fun to make and involve a lot of practical science. Ask the children to make paper darts along the lines suggested overleaf. Try to improve and alter flight patterns. An old telephone directory is a good source of paper of a constant size. Paper-clips can be added to provide weight.

Recording

Remember to record the results of each test as you go along and to discuss the results. When we say a dart flies well, what do we mean? Consider the distance flown, its speed, and its flight pattern.

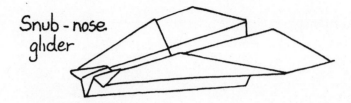

Snub-nose glider

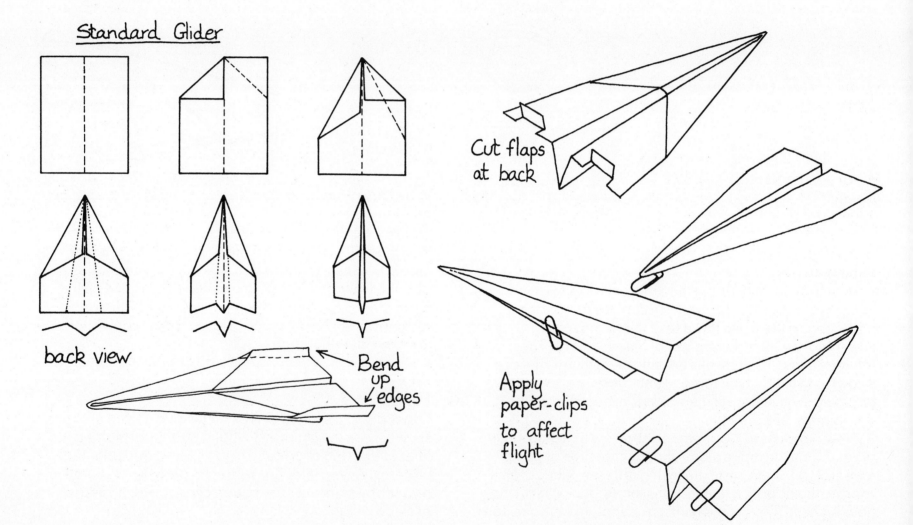

Standard Glider

back view

Bend up edges

Cut flaps at back

Apply paper-clips to affect flight

Free fall

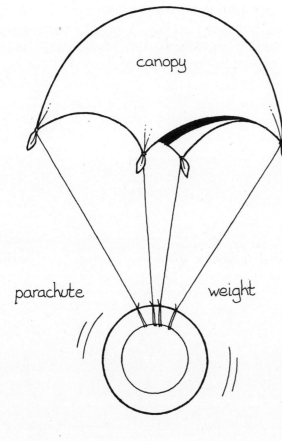

canopy

parachute

weight

Age range
Five to eleven.

Group size
Whole class.

What you need
Weights,
cotton thread,
cotton cloth,
other fabrics and
paper materials,
testing charts.

What to do
Set the children the challenge of making a parachute that falls as slowly as possible. It may help to discuss materials and shapes beforehand. Try using tissue, cellophane, plastic, cotton sheeting, etc. Test how well each one falls. Does the *size* of the canopy make a difference? Try cutting different sizes of canopy from the same material. How can the parachute be improved?

Recording
Record the results on charts.

Air power

uncontrolled flight

cotton

drinking straw

tape

long balloon

controlled flight

Age range
Five to eleven.

Group size
Small groups or whole class.

What you need
Balloons,
carpet tacks,
felt-tipped pen top,
balsa,
polystyrene meat trays,
cotton,
drinking straws,
sticky tape,
wire,
waterproof glue.

What to do

If the children blow up a balloon and release it, it will fly all over the place before it deflates. Why? Try and control the path the balloon takes. The children will enjoy making the model shown at the bottom of page 45.

Recording

Investigate how well the balloon travels. Does it need to be blown up to its maximum to make it travel the furthest? Try this out and record the results.

Follow-up 1

Ask the children if they can control the speed at which the air leaves an inflated balloon. They could try using a felt-tipped pen top with a hole made in it.

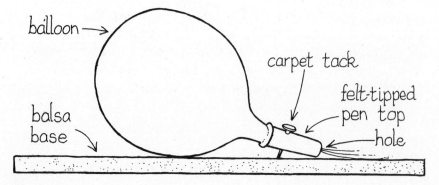

Follow-up 2

The children can now make a model that will travel using the balloon's power. Polystyrene trays used for packaging meat in supermarkets provide useful bases. The diagrams below offer possible solutions.

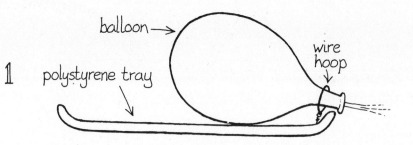

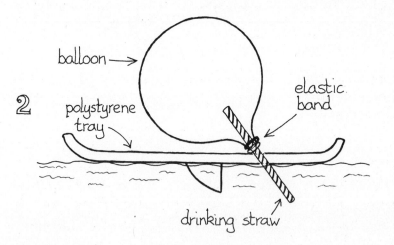

Recording

When the children have built their models, ask them to test them for speed and distance travelled. Record all their results.

Hovercraft

Age range
Seven to eleven.

Group size
Pairs or small groups.

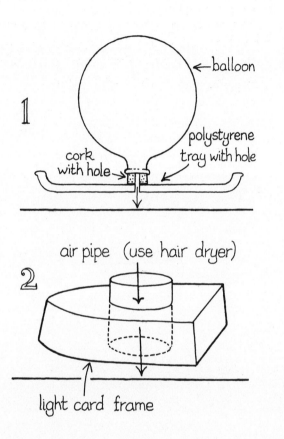

1 ←balloon

cork with hole

polystyrene tray with hole

2 air pipe (use hair dryer)

light card frame

What you need
Balloons,
corks,
polystyrene trays,
glue,
card,
hair drier.

What to do
Discuss air 'lift' with the children – how a draught will raise the edge of a rug. A hovercraft works on the same principle. Try making one that works. The diagrams shown here may help.

Recording
Test the models you have made and record the results. How long will they stay up?

Kites

polystyrene tile

button

coloured paper

heavy-duty thread passes through holes and is tied to flat buttons in upper side.

Age range
Five to eleven.

Group size
Individuals or small groups.

What you need
Polystyrene tile,
heavy-duty thread,
flat buttons,
paper.

What to do
Perhaps the most enjoyable of all flight experiments are those arising from making kites. It is possible to make a kite from a simple polystyrene tile. Designs of all kinds are to be found in books about kites. Experiment with and improve the kites using different materials.

Recording
Record the results and make diagrams of the designs.

WONDERFUL YOU

Starter

Age range
Five to eleven.

Group size
Whole class.

What you need
Coloured chalks,
large sheets
of paper.

Young children have a natural curiosity about themselves:
their height, weight, hair and eye colour, their birthday,
who can run fastest, and so on. This interest offers
numerous opportunities for scientific investigations which
can entail questioning, measuring, carrying out tests,
recording and communicating findings.

What to do
Study of the human body frequently arises from
spontaneous interest shown by a single child or group.
There is no set starting point, but in the first instance it is
probably best to consider the body as a whole. Remember
that individual children may have particular problems,
requiring a sensitive approach.

Games which involve the children sorting themselves
into different categories are a useful and popular start
with both younger and older children. On the floor of the
classroom, hall or playground, draw two chalk circles in
different colours. Then ask the children to put themselves
in one group or the other – for example, girls in the blue
circle, boys in the green.

Change the criteria for the two sets. You could use curly
or straight hair; long or short hair; blue or brown eyes;
people who like milk, people who don't. The children can
suggest categories themselves. The number of sets may
need to be increased.

Recording
Some of the examples can be recorded pictorially,
displayed and discussed. The results will show children
the characteristics they share.

Statistics

Age range
Five to eleven.

Group size
Whole class.

What you need
Drawing paper,
graph paper,
pencils,
tape-measures,
scales,
testing charts,
clipboards.

graph: eye colour.

No. Children	Blue	Brown	Others
9			
8			
7			
6			
5			
4			
3			
2			
1			

graph: shoe sizes

No. Children	Size 11	Size 12	Size 13	Size 1	Others
6					
5		👞			
4		👞			
3	👞	👞			
2	👞	👞	👞		👞
1	👞	👞	👞	👞	👞

Continue analysing categories within the class, with a greater emphasis on measuring and recording.

What to do
Ask the children to investigate some of the following categories: the number of girls in the class compared with the number of boys; how they travel to school; who is right-handed, who left-handed; eye colour; shoe size. Children will make their own suggestions for investigations. Let them follow up some of these.

Recording
These investigations can be approached in more ways than one, but it is best if the children find their own way of recording findings. You may, however, wish to stipulate what kind of graph, diagram or chart is to be made. Test charts and clipboards will no doubt be required, and the results will make a good display for others to see.

Measurement

Age range
Seven to eleven.

Group size
Pairs.

What you need
Tape-measures,
scales,
testing charts,
clipboards.

measuring around waist

measuring height

measuring weight

Encourage children to look at different categories of measurement and the relationships between them.

What to do

The children can measure each others' height, weight and waist measurements. Measure the span of hands and the armspan – the distance between the fingertips of outstretched arms.

Recording

Record the results on testing charts and compare the findings. Are taller people always heavier than shorter people? Are the thinnest people the smallest? Do tall people have longer backs than short people? Are people with the longest legs always the tallest? Compare height with armspan and hand span with arm length.

Follow-up

Ask the children to investigate the area of their feet and hands. This can be done by drawing around them on squared paper and counting the squares. Count half-squares – over half, take as a whole square, under half, take as none. It is not essential to use square centimetres as units.

Can the children suggest any ways of finding out the area of their whole skin? Possibilities include drawing around front, back and sides on squared paper, or making cylinders around trunk, arms, legs, head and neck, and so calculating the total area.

Body skills

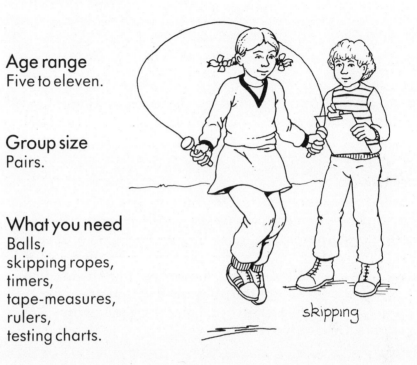

skipping

Age range

Five to eleven.

Group size

Pairs.

What you need

Balls,
skipping ropes,
timers,
tape-measures,
rulers,
testing charts.

Many children like to know who does what best – but they are not always clear about what they mean by best, and their tests are not always fair. Encourage them to devise tests which will help them to find out about their own bodies. Try to include investigations which allow the less physically able children to do well.

What to do

Can the children test the ball skills suggested on page 19? Other skills might include skipping, jumping, running and similar playground activities. Remember, they must decide what is being tested: the number of skips in 20 seconds, or the time taken to do 20 skips.

Recording
The children should record results, represent them in diagram or graph form, and then try to explain their findings to each other.

Follow-up
Testing reflexes can be fun. It is best done in pairs. One person holds a ruler upright with zero at the bottom. The other person holds their index finger and thumb around the ruler (not touching it) at the zero mark. The first person drops the ruler suddenly, and the partner must try to catch it. Number one records the point at which the ruler was caught. Repeat the test several times and then swap partners. Discuss the results.

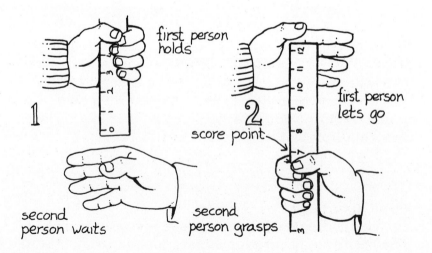

Mapping a hand

Age range
Five to eleven.

Group size
Whole class.

What you need
Ink pad,
fingerprint charts,
paper.

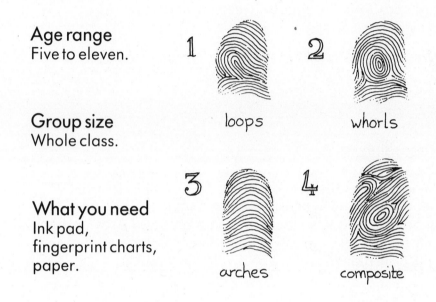

What to do
Copy the fingerprint charts from page 120, and encourage the children to examine and investigate their fingerprints. These can best be made by rolling the finger lightly from one side to the other – first on the ink pad, and then on the paper, thus elongating the pattern made. Use washable ink. Ask the children to look for loops (1), whorls (2), arches (3) and composites (4). A mirror can be used for making rather less messy fingerprints.

Recording
Do all your fingers make the same prints? Do all boys have the same prints? Do all index fingers make the same

sort of print? Questions based upon the records made should encourage children to widen their investigations.

Follow-up
Individuals can copy on to paper the line patterns of their palms, and then compare them with those of others in their group. Ask them to look for regularly-occurring lines and try to explain these.

Using hands

Age range
Five to nine.

Group size
Small groups or whole class.

What you need
Paper,
washable paint,
pens,
bottle or rolling pin,
table top or Formica
surface.

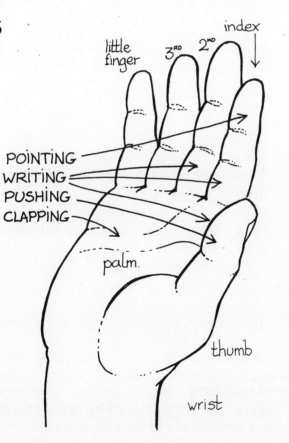

What to do
Get the children talking about hands and what we can do with them. Here are some suggestions they might offer: hold, grip, grasp, push, pull, clasp, draw, paint, write, tickle, poke, pinch, slap, punch, clap, shake hands, wave, scratch. Which parts of the hand are used for which activity? See if they can guess correctly.

Recording
Make hand prints with washable paint on paper. Cut them out and label the different parts.

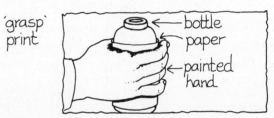

Follow-up
A group can try making 'grasp' prints. A hand is covered in washable paint and grips a milk bottle or rolling pin covered in paper. Does this print look the same as the flat one? How is it different?

Investigate ways in which we can paint using our hands: holding a paint brush in the normal way; finger painting (drawing with a finger dipped in paint); tracing a picture with a finger in an area of paper already spread with paint; using fingers as print makers.

Children may like to paint their fingers with paint sticks and use them as puppets.

53

Feelies

Age range
Five to nine.

Group size
Small group or
whole class.

What you need
Cardboard box
or draw-string bag,
items for 'feely' box,
testing charts.

What to do
Start a discussion about feeling things. What do we use to
feel things? Fingers . . . Can we feel with other parts of the
body? Which?

Make a 'feely' box or bag. This can be a simple
cardboard box with armholes cut in it, or a bag with a
draw-string. Put in a selection of objects of varying shape,
size and texture. Encourage the children to talk about
these as they explore each item, *without* at first naming
them. The words they use might include phrases such as:
damp, dry, angles, flat surface, regular or not, smooth,
sticky, bumpy, tickly, stretchy. Ask questions: would it
float? Would it break easily? Does it crumble in the hand?

If you have a set of Treesorts or Housesorts, put these in
the box. Which attributes can the children identify? Which
are they unable to identify?

Follow-up
Individuals can choose ten items to put in the box and ask
friends to try and identify them. Jelly cubes, peeled
grapes, wet spaghetti and toothbrushes make good
starters! Ask the children to find out whether they are
better using their right or their left hand. What about
their feet?

Recording
Record the accuracy of the children's predictions and the
words they use to describe objects.

Footprints

Age range
Five to eleven.

Group size
Individuals or small group.

What you need
Paper (black and white),
washable paint,
shallow tin,
sponge,
talcum powder,
sand,
testing chart,
tape-measure.

What to do
Footprints make an interesting study. They can be made in several ways: with wet feet on a dry floor; with washable paint on paper; in damp sand; by dipping the feet in talc and stepping on black paper. Ask the children to make some footprints and then encourage them to ask questions about them. Is the print flat or dented? Which parts of the foot touch the ground? What happens when you walk, hop, stand, squat, stand on tiptoe? Are all prints alike? How do they differ?

Recording
Children can measure the length and area of their print.

Follow-up
Ask individuals to run along a strip of paper with painted feet and look at the patterns made. They can try to explain the differences in prints. They can also examine their stride length when walking, running and hopping. One person could invent a sequence of movements: for example, run four, walk two, stand, walk two, crouch. Then ask others in the group if they can identify the sequence from the prints made.

Peep toe

Age range
Five to eleven.

Group size
Small groups or whole class.

What you need
Blanket,
paper,
ink pad,
testing charts.

What to do
Ask the children if they can tell the difference between girls' and boys' feet. They probably think they can, so put them to the test. Hang a blanket in the doorway so that it touches the floor. Have two people outside as testers. Other members of the class poke their feet under the blanket in turn. It's a lot of fun – but the class must be carefully controlled!

Recording
The two outside must record the results. How many times were they right? What made them decide whether it was a boy or a girl?

Follow-up
Individuals may measure the length of their toes and compare the results with other members of the class. Does the person with the longest toes have the longest foot?

A group may like to examine toe prints in the same way as fingerprints. Children can also study toe and nail shapes and the line patterns on the soles of the feet. Suggest they draw some of their observations.

Seeing in the dark

Age range
Seven to eleven.

Group size
Pairs or small groups.

What you need

Chalk,
pencils,
paper,
graph paper,
blindfold,
blankets.

blindfold

What to do

Ask the children why we need eyes: to gain information; (Who? What? Where?); to make judgements (Will it fit? Can we eat it?); to enjoy things. Can they think of any examples?

Make a dark area in a cupboard or under a table using blankets or curtains. How well can they see when they first enter? Does this improve after a time? Ask a group to find the darkest place in the classroom or playground and explain their choice.

Follow-up

The children might like to discover how well they can find their way around the class blindfolded. Can they walk in a straight line forwards and backwards? One person could try walking blindfolded along the edge of a netball court marking line (or something similar) whilst a partner maps their progress with chalk. Careful supervision is required to ensure safety and to prevent foul play!

Light and sight

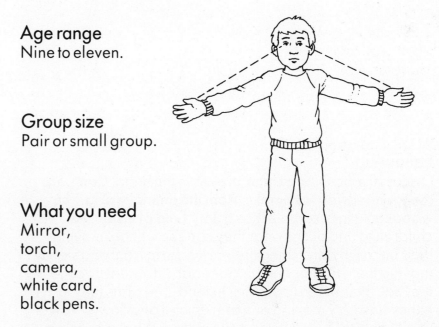

Age range

Nine to eleven.

Group size

Pair or small group.

What you need

Mirror,
torch,
camera,
white card,
black pens.

What to do

Ask children to look at their eyes in a mirror and watch what happens when a bright light from a torch is shone into one eye. **Supervise this experiment very carefully.** What happens if they then look at a black surface? Can they try to explain this?

Talk about the structure of the eye, and how it works. Then ask them to look again and watch the dilation or contraction of the iris to alter pupil size. Show children the mechanism of the lens and shutter of an empty camera. If the children close one eye and gently place their fingertip on the lid, they will feel the cornea (the eye's main focusing lens) as the eye moves to and fro. **Again, supervise them with the greatest attention.**

Follow-up 1
Discuss the position of human eyes in the head. Compare them with various examples from the animal world. The woodcock, for example, has a 360° field of vision. Ask children to find out how far they can see without moving their heads, by stretching their arms out in front and slowly moving them further and further apart. How easily can they see their fingertips if they extend their arms fully to either side? Try moving one arm up and one down. Now what happens? Try with one eye closed. What difference does this make?

Which eye do you use the most? With both eyes open, children can line up a pencil with a corner of the room. They should then close one eye at a time and see in which direction the pencil appears to move. Normally the pencil will appear to jump to one side when one eye is closed. This is the eye that is used the most — ie, the dominant eye.

Recording
A group can investigate how many have a dominant right or left eye, and record results.

which eye is dominant?

corner →

Follow-up 2
Ask the children to investigate blinking. They can try to explain why we do this. Can they look at each other without blinking? For how long? How many times can they deliberately blink within ten seconds? Make five white cards 20×20 cm, each with a different-sized black dot in the centre. Ask the children to see how far away they can get before they lose sight of the dots. Work in pairs and make a fair test of it. Who has the best vision?

Smell

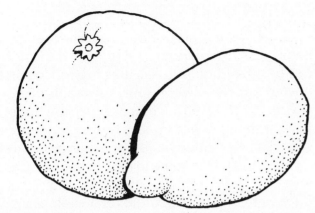

Age range
Five to nine.

Group size
Whole class.

What you need
Yoghurt pots,
nylon,
rubber bands,
orange or lemon,
chocolate,
coffee,
soap,
pine cones,
lavender or mint,
herbs and spices.

smell pots   nylon cover

rubber band   yoghurt pot

	A	B	C	D	E
David	✓	✓	✗	✓	
Sophie	✗	✗	✓	✗	
Peter	✓	✗	✓	✓	
Sally	✓	✓	✓	✓	

What to do
Smell jars can be made from yoghurt pots, covered in
nylon from dark tights secured by a rubber band. Provide
a variety of items for the children to smell, remembering to
make a key for identification. The pots should be marked
with letters or numbers. Can the children guess the
contents correctly?

Recording
Ask the children to record their results in any way they can,
and try to explain why different people get different
results.

Follow-up 1
How long does a smell last? Get the children to dip their
fingers into cologne or eat an orange. Is the smell still
there after 15 minutes/30 minutes/one hour? Can we smell
something when it is under water? Ask the children to
investigate . . .

Follow-up 2
Play a game of 'follow your nose': hide three or four items.
Who can find them by their smell? Ask the children if they
can find out what is for school lunch without seeing the
food. They must not ask anyone, go into the kitchen, or
look at a menu!

Taste

yoghurt pots

tongue map ↓

Age range
Five to nine.

Group size
Small or medium groups.

What you need
Blindfold,
yoghurt pots,
paper,
flour,
salt,
cornflour,
icing sugar,
custard
powder.

substances correctly by dipping their fingers in and tasting? You might try: flour, salt, sherbet, cornflour, icing sugar, custard powder . . . Number the pots and make a key for identification. Ask the children to sort the tastes into categories: sweet, sour, salty, bitter.

Can the children tell margarine from butter? Let them taste samples on toothpicks and say which is which. Try salted and unsalted butter, or perhaps home-made butter — you could make some in the classroom. Other consumer tests are useful. Ask the children to sample and grade different kinds of chocolate for sweetness; or different brands of crisps for saltiness. Provide a selection of flavoured crisps in plain bags. Can the children identify the different flavours?

Follow-up
Can the children locate the sensitive parts of the tongue? Try placing a pinch of icing sugar on different parts of the tongue until they are identified. Try with salt, lemon and bitter chocolate. The individual should be blindfolded. Try mixing two kinds of flavour — eg sugar in vinegar. Does the mixture taste sweet or sour? Where on the tongue can they taste it?

What to do
Have a tasting session: lay out a selection of white powders in yoghurt pots. Can the children identify the

Recording
Ask them to record and explain their results, and then draw a 'tongue map', showing the sensitive areas.

Hearing 1

Age range
Five to nine.

Group size
Whole class.

What you need
Paper,
clipboards,
tape recorder,
shaker pots or tins,
blindfold,
handbell, triangle
or small drum.

What to do
From how far away can you hear a sound? Ask the children to investigate this and record the results. They could use a drum or a bell to make the sound; make sure

that the rest of the school – or neighbourhood – is not unduly disturbed! What is the greatest distance from which you can hear the noise?

Ask the children to sit still and to listen very carefully. What can they hear? Can they tell what is making each sound? A small group can go on a 'listening walk' around the school and record (in whatever way they wish) the sounds heard.

Make a 'sounds' tape; you could include a telephone, a doorbell, a tap dripping, a police siren, a cry or scream, a whistle, somebody laughing. What does each sound tell us? How is it made?

Have 'shaker pots' filled with different items (tobacco tins are ideal). Try crumpled paper, pencils, marbles, sand, coins, feathers. Can the children guess what's inside? Number the shaker pots and make a key for identification.

Follow-up
Can the children locate sounds accurately? They should work in pairs. One sits blindfolded in a chair, head facing forwards. Their partner plays a note on a triangle or rings a handbell in various positions: directly in front, to the right and left, behind, above or below head level. The person sitting down points to the source of the sound. Which are the best positions to hear from, and which are the worst? Which child is the most successful at locating sounds?

Hearing 2

card →

ear trumpet

Age range
Nine to eleven.

Group size
Small groups.

What you need
Tape-measure,
testing charts,
wax ear-plugs,
thin card,
yoghurt pots,
string,
clock.

string

yoghurt pot

string telephone

What to do
It is fun to try to see if hearing can be improved by using
ear-trumpets – cones made of thin card. Ask the children
to measure how far they can walk from a clock and still
hear it ticking. Then they should try with the ear-trumpet.
Does it make a difference?

Does everyone have equally good hearing? Investigate
this. A group could devise tests, and then rank themselves
in order of hearing ability. They may wish to try the same
tests using only one ear (decide which). Wax ear-plugs are
very effective in blotting out the sound in one ear – but only
use them with careful supervision. Can individuals find out
whether each of their ears has equally good hearing?

Recording
Record the results on testing charts.

Follow-up
String telephones are always fun to make and use.
Children can be encouraged to improve on their original
model. They must try to build the most efficient machine
they can. How important is the length of string? Suggest
that individuals try putting the knot on the ear side only.
Does this make it work better? Why?

Heart, pulse, lungs

Age range
Nine to eleven.

Group size
Small groups.

What you need
Seconds timer, testing chart.

feel pulse here

What to do
Get the children to investigate their heartbeats after strenuous exercise, and under normal conditions as well. How many times do their hearts beat in 15 seconds? Can they find their pulse? How many times do they beat in a minute? **Careful supervision is necessary.**

Recording
Record the results for the group. Ask children to make a graph of the pulse rates of various individuals, and then investigate how these change with exercise. Can they explain what happens? Whose pulse changes the least?

Whose the most? These results can then be compared with those for the breathing rate (see page 37).

Follow-up
During exercise, children can also look for other changes in the body. These may include panting, sweating and colour changes. Talk about these changes with them, and suggest they try to find out more from the school library.

Body records
At the start and end of each term children can fill in their own body charts. These can be copied from page 119. They can see who has grown most, or least, and where*. They can also try to find average growth rates and see how and where the body changes at their age. These facts and figures could be stored on the BBC *Factfile* program for the BBC microcomputer. Similar data storage software is available for other machines. (*Be aware of potential embarrassment for pubescent children.)

REFLECTIONS

Starter

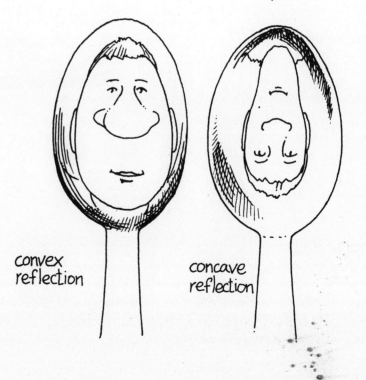

Age range
Five to eleven.

Group size
Whole class.

What you need
Paper,
mirrors,
balls,
polished spoon.

What to do
Ask the children to try bouncing sunlight on to the ceiling by using a mirror. They can play a game chasing each others' dots around. When they have practised they can draw a target on the wall and have a competition to see who is the most accurate.

Light bounces off mirrors in much the same way as a ball bounces from a smooth surface. When the surface is rough, the bounce is unpredictable; similarly, light reflected from a rough surface is broken up unevenly.

Follow-up
Ask the children to see what they look like when reflected in a polished spoon. Explain that concave means bending in and convex means bending out.

Recording
The children can draw the outline of the spoon on paper, and sketch in their appearance on the concave side of the spoon and the convex. Ask them to try to explain their findings.

spoons

convex
reflection

concave
reflection

Mirror images

Age range
Five to nine.

Group size
Small group or whole class.

What you need
Mirrors,
blotting paper,
ink pens,
ink,
drawing paper.

What to do
Ask the children to look in a mirror. Then they should wink an eye. Which eye do they see wink in the mirror? Can they see what is behind them? By moving the angle of the mirror they will be able to get a view of their surroundings in the mirror. Can they explain why?

Follow-up 1
Ask individuals to write something on a piece of paper with an ink pen. Then quickly blot it with clean blotting paper. By using a mirror can they now read what is written on the blotting paper?

Recording
They can then try writing in mirror writing and sending messages to each other.

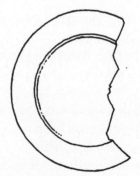

Follow-up 2
Ask the children to use a mirror to 'mend' the broken plate on the left. Can they make a 'tree' out of the plate on the right? What kind of a tree is it? They should record where they place the mirror.

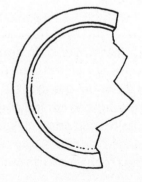

Changing directions

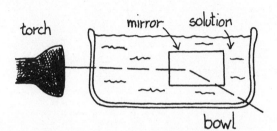

Age range
Seven to eleven.

Group size
Pair or small group.

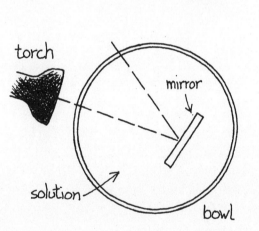

What you need
Transparent bowl,
mirrors,
torch,
card,
masking tape,
ruler.

What to do
Most children have used a mirror and seen their reflection, but they may not realize that mirrors can also change the direction of light. Tape over a torch front so that it emits only a single, narrow beam of light. Ask the children to find a darkish corner and try shining the torch into a transparent bowl of milk and water containing a mirror. They will be able to see how the light changes direction. Can they try to find a way of measuring the angle of reflection?

Follow-up
Suggest the children try to make a periscope using a ruler, some Plasticine and two mirrors. To make it work they will have to adjust the angle of the mirrors. At what angle should the mirrors be placed?

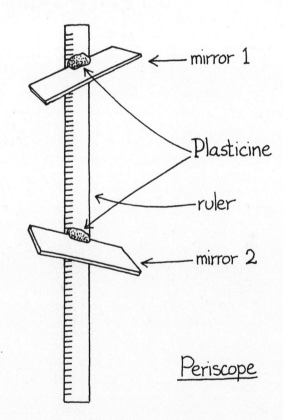

Periscope

Recording
The children can draw a diagram of the periscope, marking in the angles.

MATERIALS

Starter

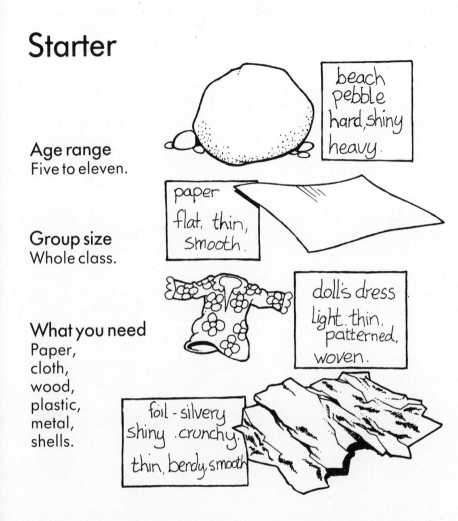

beach pebble hard, shiny heavy.

paper flat, thin, smooth.

doll's dress light, thin, patterned, woven.

foil - silvery shiny, crunchy, thin, bendy, smooth

Age range
Five to eleven.

Group size
Whole class.

What you need
Paper,
cloth,
wood,
plastic,
metal,
shells.

This is a very valuable exercise in sorting and grouping. It will stimulate children and encourage spontaneous study.

What to do
A very good way to start a topic on materials is for the children to make collections of different kinds: wood, plastic, cloth, metal, stones and rocks, shells, paper, etc.

The children can sort and group them. This can be done by size, shape, colour, texture, use. Alternatively, they could be grouped according to whether they are natural or artificial – ie living, once living, or never living. The children should be encouraged to feel and touch materials, and to describe them verbally.

Recording
The materials can be displayed on the wall or on tables. The children could attach a descriptive label to each one. Older children will be able to formalize the sets they have grouped together in Venn diagram form.

Sizing of paper

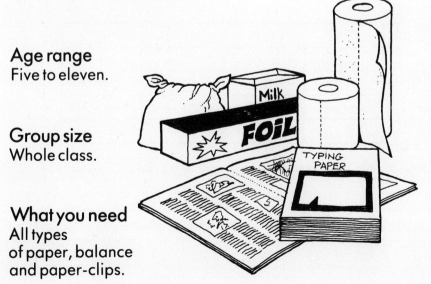

Age range
Five to eleven.

Group size
Whole class.

What you need
All types
of paper, balance
and paper-clips.

What to do

The children can collect as many different kinds of paper as they can find: newspaper, tissue, sugar paper, wrapping paper, greaseproof paper, writing paper, carbon paper, foil, card, envelopes, wrappers. Let them tell you what they think each kind of paper is used for. Talk about the thickness of the paper and the way it is made. The children can weigh the different papers using paper-clips instead of weights.

Ask them to measure paper to see if any sizes occur regularly. Don't tell them; let them find out. Talk about standardizing sizes. Remember that this page is A4; half this size is A5; twice its size is A3, and so on, up to A1.

Recording

The different papers should be listed and described on a testing chart, and their sizes and weights written in.

paper	width.	length.	weight
1 (tracing)	21 cm.	15 cm	1 paper-clip
2 (drawing)	42 cm.	15 cm	5 paper-clips
3 (writing)	21 cm.	15 cm	2 paper-clips
4 (tissue)	28 cm.	30 cm	1 paper-clip

Paper: wear and tear

Age range
Five to eleven.

Group size
Small groups.

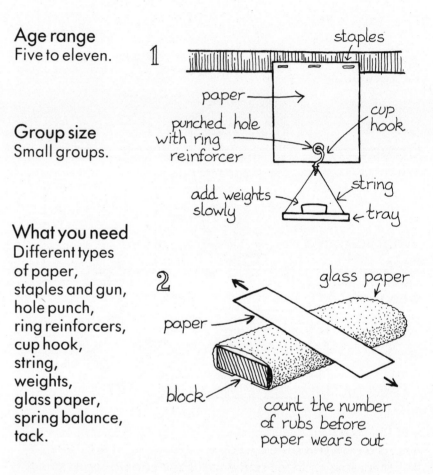

1 — staples, paper, punched hole with ring reinforcer, cup hook, add weights slowly, string, tray

2 — paper, glass paper, block, count the number of rubs before paper wears out

What you need
Different types of paper, staples and gun, hole punch, ring reinforcers, cup hook, string, weights, glass paper, spring balance, tack.

What to do
It soon becomes obvious to the children that different types of paper have different qualities. Ask them to find out which paper is best for writing on with a pen? Which paper is strongest? Does 'strong' mean that it takes a lot of

rubbing, or that it does not tear easily? Grade papers accordingly. Does the order change when the paper is wet?

In attempting to answer these questions, the children will have to form theories about each kind of paper, and then devise their own tests. The diagrams above may serve as examples. Point out that manufacturers need to do similar tests when deciding which paper to use for a job.

Recording
Record all the results on testing charts and then discuss and explain them.

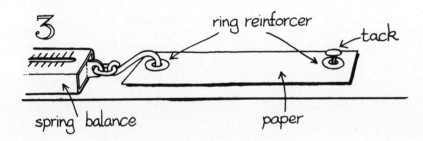

3

ring reinforcer

tack

spring balance

paper

Follow-up 1
How many times can you fold a piece of paper in half? Does it depend on the size of the paper? Is paper which is of double thickness twice as strong?

Follow-up 2
Children will notice that paper creases a great deal. Study the 'crumple factor': by how much does a piece of paper

appear to shrink, having been screwed up and then opened out again? Talk about surface area and how it appears to alter.

Recording
Record the results on a testing chart. Start with pieces of paper of an equal size and screw them up with the same pressure.

Wet paper

Age range
Five to eleven.

Group size
Small groups.

What you need
Absorbent papers,
water-resistant
papers,
water,
tray,
ink,
pegs,
glass jars,
rubber bands,
spoon/straw/
pipettes,
stop-watch.

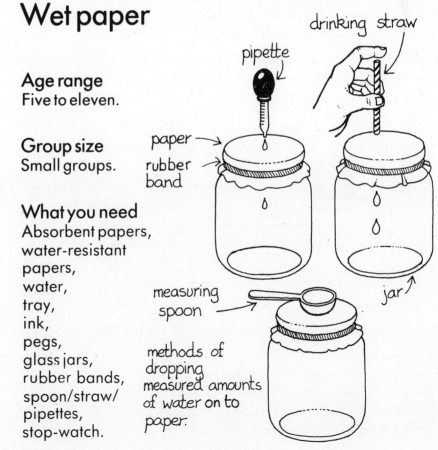

pipette

drinking straw

paper

rubber band

jar

measuring spoon

methods of dropping measured amounts of water on to paper.

What to do
Can the children devise fair tests for absorbency? A possible example might look like the one below.

Recording
The children must establish criteria first. What do they intend to measure? The height the dampness reaches in 30 seconds? How long the paper takes to soak up five centimetres? How far the water travels if it is left? Or how much water is soaked up? If they add dye or ink to the water, they will be able to use the paper itself as the record, perhaps mounted on graph paper.

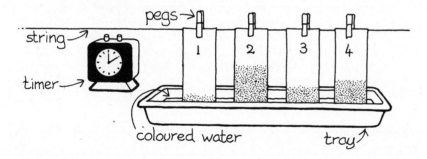

Follow-up
Some papers need to be water resistant or waterproof. Measured amounts of water can be released on to paper by the methods shown on page 71. Test fairly and methodically.

Fixing paper

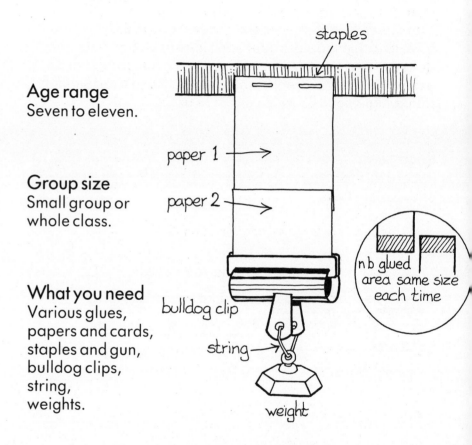

Age range
Seven to eleven.

Group size
Small group or whole class.

What you need
Various glues, papers and cards, staples and gun, bulldog clips, string, weights.

This is another informative topic which has scope for practical experimentation.

What to do
Get the children to think of ways of holding paper together. How is glue made? How well does it work compared with paste, staples, pins, tags, etc? They

should be thinking about strength, reliability, speed, ease of use . . . Ask them to list all the glues found in school and to identify for what each is used. The children can set about devising tests to see which glue is strongest. Do some papers stick together better than others? Ensure that the glued area of overlap is the same each time. **Be aware of the dangers of sniffing.**

Follow-up
Carry out similar comparative tests for other materials and other fasteners and fixers.

Recording
Use testing charts to record results of tests.

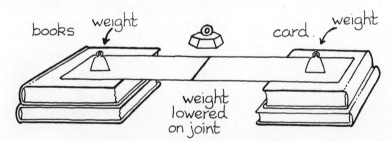

glue	materials
UHU	wood, paper, plastic
Cow	paper.
Evostik	metals, plastic, wood.
	paper, fabric,
Britfix	plastics.

Clothes

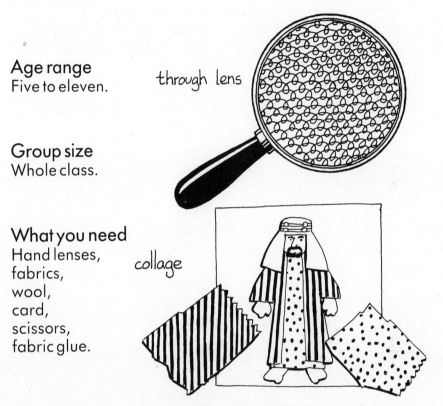

through lens

collage

Age range
Five to eleven.

Group size
Whole class.

What you need
Hand lenses,
fabrics,
wool,
card,
scissors,
fabric glue.

What to do
An easy way to start an investigation into clothing materials is to examine through a hand lens knitted and woven fabrics that the children are wearing. They will see that woven fabrics are intertwined, whilst knitted fabrics are looped together. Compare these materials with compressed fabrics such as felt. Most textiles consist of cloth around holes. It is important to point this out to children. The holes trap pockets of air which the body makes warm – thus providing warm clothing. If you can

73

get some scraps of fabric, let the children fray the ends to see how it is made.

Talk about costumes and clothes from different countries. Arabs wear long, loose robes to keep them cool: the movement of air produces draughts. Eskimos use animal furs for warmth. Children can draw pictures of them and explain why they wear such clothes. Children may like to dress figures collage-style for hot, cold or rainy days, using appropriate materials.

Discuss the following questions: why do we wear particular clothes? When do we wear them? For going out in the rain, swimming, dancing, playing sports, sleeping, etc. Talk about special clothes worn for special jobs.

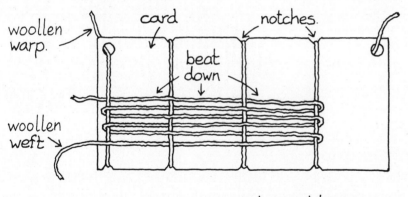

a simple card loom.

Follow-up
The children can try weaving and knitting for themselves.

74

Warm and dry

Age range
Nine to eleven.

Group size
Small groups.

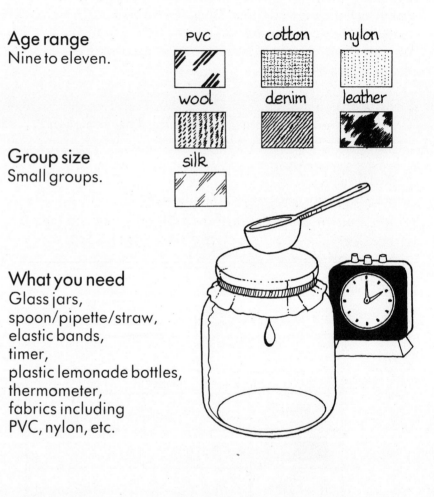

What you need
Glass jars,
spoon/pipette/straw,
elastic bands,
timer,
plastic lemonade bottles,
thermometer,
fabrics including
PVC, nylon, etc.

What to do
Ask the children which material is best for keeping dry on rainy days. Collect together small pieces of various fabrics, say in 20-centimetre squares. Fasten them over a

series of jars by means of an elastic band. Drop a measured amount of water on each as on page 71. On which jar does the water soak through the quickest? Which is the best fabric for keeping water out? Repeat the test; is the result the same this time? Does fabric that is already wet let water through more easily?

Follow-up
Ask them which fabrics are good for keeping us warm. A simple test will give us some answers. The children should wrap plastic lemonade bottles in different fabrics: cotton [sheeting]; [petticoat] nylon; woollen blanket; woollen jumper; fur; PVC. Leave one bottle uncovered. Fill each bottle with hot water and leave them for 30 minutes. Which is warmest? Take the temperature. Leave them for a further 30 minutes and test again. How does each one compare with the uncovered bottle?

Recording
Record all the results for both experiments on testing charts. Investigate the results.

Testing fabrics

Age range
Nine to eleven.

Group size
Whole class.

What you need
Fabrics,
staples and gun,
ruler,
weights,
spring balance,
yoghurt pot,
string.

What to do
The children can now talk about other fabric properties: strength, stretch, wear, shrinkage, tearing, how well it absorbs dye, etc. The children should collect different kinds of fabric and group them in sets. Again, emphasize the difference between synthetic and natural fibres; discuss how nylon, rayon, etc, are made.

Recording

The groupings can be displayed in chart form, in sets, or in columns.

Follow-up

Suggest that the whole class becomes a clothing factory. The children will need to establish which fabrics are suitable for certain garments: T-shirts, for example, will need to stretch well and be comfortable; trousers will need to be hard-wearing.

Let the children devise their own tests. This will involve forming theories and making sure that the tests are fair. This may mean that fabric samples will have to be cut to standard sizes, say 20×10 centimetres. Fabrics might be tested in the same way as the paper in the second diagram on page 70, or as in the picture below. With the stretch test, children must first establish criteria. Are they finding out how much stretch three kilograms will produce, or how much weight causes a three-centimetre stretch?

The children can try tearing fabrics and then invent a test to see how easily a fabric will tear – perhaps something on the lines shown below. It is sometimes best to 'help' the tear with a small nick in the side, provided each fabric gets the same treatment.

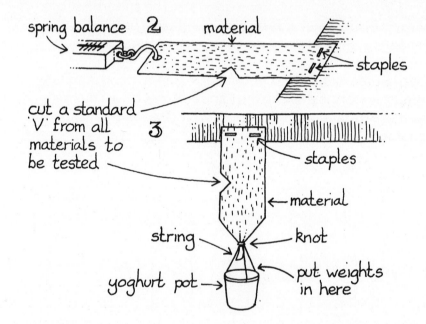

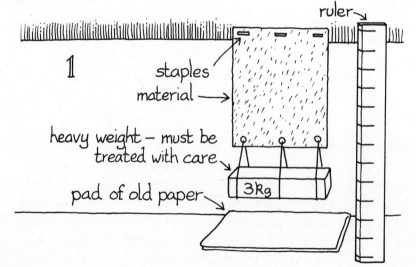

Recording

The results should be recorded on testing charts, and then taken to the 'factory managers' for approval. Which materials will they select, and why?

Washing and shrinking

Age range
Seven to eleven.

Group size
Small groups.

What you need
Bowls,
washing powder,
clothes-line and pegs,
hot and cold water,
fabrics,
testing charts.

What to do
Can the children bring from home a garment that has obviously shrunk? It will cause some amusement! Why do fabrics shrink?

Using pieces of material cut to the same size, the children can wash them in hot and in cold water, measuring the fabrics before and after the test. Do certain fabrics shrink when dried over a radiator, but not when dried in the wind? Does the fabric lose its shape? Which fabric holds its shape best? Does hot or cold water cause more shrinkage? Do different fabrics wash better at different water temperatures? Further investigations might make washing powder a variable in addition to water; and different materials can be tested for their dyefast properties. Try crêpe paper as one sample.

Recording
Graphs and diagrams represent the results of the tests very well, but all kinds of imaginative displays can be made using the fabrics themselves.

Follow-up
Suggest that children look at the labels in clothes; most have washing instructions. Discuss the differences between hand- and machine-washable fabrics, and soap powder and detergent. Children may like to write washing instructions for the fabrics they have tested, using symbols they have seen on clothing labels, or devising their own.

Collecting stones

Age range
Five to seven.

Group size
Small groups or whole class.

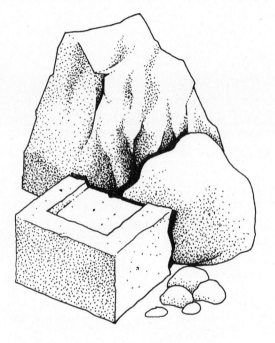

What you need
Assorted stones, scales, callipers, rulers, clipboards, testing charts.

What to do
The children can make a collection of stones, having first decided what counts as one. (What about brick? Pieces of coal? Things made from stone, such as chalk?) Take the children out to look for a variety of colours, sizes, shapes and textures. Ask the children to bring stones back when they go on holiday – perhaps accompanied by a postcard, which will make an attractive display.

Encourage the children to sort and group the stones into sets: for example shiny/dull, rough/smooth, rounded/sharp, hard/soft. Or they may use colour, weight and size as criteria. Do the biggest stones always weigh the most? Can you tell if a stone is heavy by looking at it? Think about porous stones such as chalk, and other kinds like beach pebbles.

Follow-up
Children may choose to select one particular stone as their special one, and then find out all about it, its weight and measurements.

Examining stones 1

Age range
Nine to seven.

Group size
Small groups or whole class.

soaking stones

What you need
Stones,
water,
graduated beaker or
displacement bucket,
scales,
testing charts,
nails.

stone	dry	after soaking
1	1kg	
2	2kg	
3	500g	

What do do
Older children who have learnt about volume and displacement may be able to find the volume of stones by using a displacement bucket, or simply by using a beaker and measuring the volume displaced by the stone. The equipment illustrated on page 18 (Fig 3) may be used. They may notice that the stone is a different colour when it is wet. Can they explain this, and investigate how stones react to water? Do any stones dissolve in water? Do any stones soak up water? If so, how much? How can you test this?

Recording
Record the results on a testing chart. Always encourage the children to put forward their own explanations.

Follow-up
The children can investigate the hardness of stones. They can scratch stones with fingernails, a nail, or other stones. Make a chart with the stones placed in order of hardness.

Examining stones 2

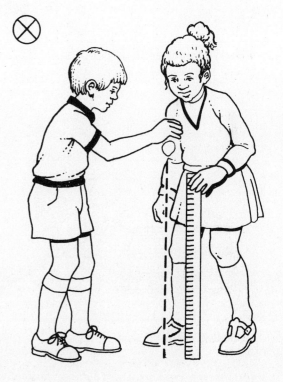

Age range
Seven to eleven.

Group size
Pairs.

What you need
Stones,
ruler,
testing charts,
books,
plank,
graph paper.

79

What to do

Ask individuals if they think a stone will roll or bounce in the playground. Can it bounce? How high? To make the tests fair, always drop the stones from the same height. Does the stone roll in a straight line? How far can you make it roll? Which stone rolls best? How can you improve its roll? If it doesn't roll, can you make it slide?

Encourage the children to investigate these possibilities; they involve a lot of measuring, recording and making comparisons. To make a stone roll further they might increase the angle of the slope or even coat the slope in soap or oil.

Recording

Tabulate the results and represent them in graph form. Always try to explain results.

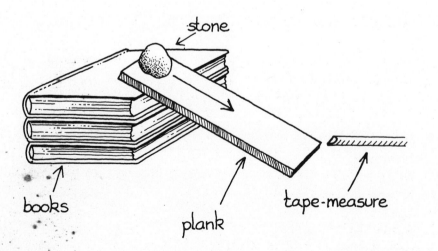

stone

books

plank

tape-measure

Building with stones

Age range
Nine to eleven.

Group size
Small groups or whole class.

What you need
Stones,
cement,
sand,
water,
wire,
thread,
straw,
plastic
supermarket trays,
weights.

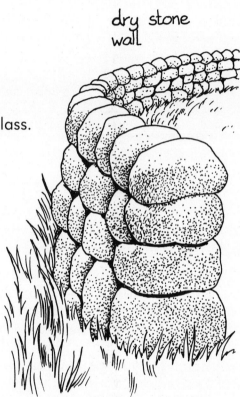

dry stone wall

What to do

Try to build a dry stone wall with the children. What problems are involved? How can they be overcome? What fixatives can the children suggest? Do they work?

Go out and look at some bricks and mortar with the children. Discuss how things are built. With cement and

mix	sand	cement
A	1	1
B	2	1
C	1	2

sand, try to mix a mortar that will hold together. Use different proportions and test each mixture for strength, brittleness and stickiness. Thin plastic supermarket trays of identical size may be used as moulds for each mixture. Hang weights upon the test pieces and keep adding more weight until they break. Try to strengthen the toughest mixture by adding pieces of wire (as in reinforced concrete), or strands of nylon (as in radial tyres), or even straw — the ancient way of making bricks in Egypt. Does the amount of water used make any difference?

Recording
Record the results of this and any other tests that the children might devise.

Stone rubbings

stone
rubbings

Age range
Five to eleven.

Group size
Whole class.

What you need
Wax crayons or cobbler's wax, paper.

Examine the special properties and uses of stone, and the ways in which it can be worked.

What to do
An excursion from school may provide opportunities to see the way in which stone can be used to provide monuments and statues. Look at stone carvings and the script used by masons. Children can make rubbings of any stone inscriptions they find. Remember to obtain permission before visiting private property, churches, churchyards, etc.

Recording
The rubbings can make an interesting classroom display.

WATER

Starter

Age range
Five to seven.

Group size
Small groups.

What you need
Water,
water trough,
plastic lemonade bottles,
jugs and containers,
waterproof markers,
elastic bands.

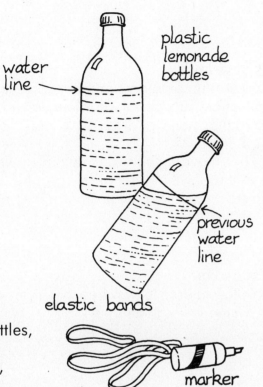

water line

plastic lemonade bottles

previous water line

elastic bands

marker

What to do
Young children enjoy spending time filling and emptying containers with water. Structure this activity by presenting them with a range of containers of various sizes and shapes, some with wide necks and others with narrow necks. Which is the easiest to fill, and why? Talk about the use of funnels, and try making one. Are the containers which can be filled the quickest also the quickest to empty?

Ask the children to pour water into transparent plastic lemonade bottles until they are half full. Screw on the caps. What happens to the surface of the water when the bottles are tilted, and when they are turned upside down?

Recording
The children should predict the water line first and then test. They could mark the position of the water line with elastic bands or with a waterproof marker.

Sink or swim

Age range
Five to nine.

Group size
Pairs.

water trough

What you need
Water trough,
washing-up bowls
or basins,
water,
objects for
sinking/floating,
paper and pens,
testing chart,
sorting hoops.

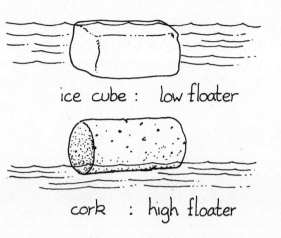

ice cube : low floater

cork : high floater

What to do
Make a collection of various objects. Include some made of metal, wood, rubber, plastic, glass, cork, sponge, expanded polystyrene, or stone. Ask the children which they think will float, and which will sink. Test each one in a water trough.

Recording
The results could be presented in several ways – by making two sets in sorting hoops, for instance. These sets could then be drawn.

Follow-up 1
Now direct the children's attention to the floaters. If they work in pairs with smaller bowls of water, they can each test how well objects float. Are they high or low in the water?

Recording
Each pair could record the position of the objects in relation to the surface of the water by making a diagram.

Follow-up 2
Add plastic containers and soft drink cans to the collection. Talk about what they are made of. What happens when they are put in water? Can the children explain why?

Then move to items which sink. The way in which they pass through the water differs greatly. Some sway from side to side, others fall straight to the bottom.

Recording
Ask the children to watch each item sink and then try to draw the sinking patterns.

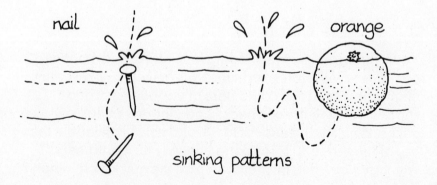

nail

orange

sinking patterns

Floating shapes

Age range
Seven to nine.

Group size
Small groups.

What you need
Water,
washing-up bowls, basins,
or water trough,
Plasticine,
Lego or something similar,
foil.

What to do
Give each of the children a lump of Plasticine. Ask them whether they think it will float or sink. It sinks! Now ask them to try to make the lump float. Let them try making different shapes. Which floats best? They should eventually discover that a coracle shape is the most efficient. Give them several lumps of the same size with which to experiment.

Recording
The children can record their results by making drawings of the side views of the boats they have made in the water.

Follow-up 1
Ask the children which boat will carry most. The cargo should be made up of standard units: marbles tend to roll out, but pieces of Lego, or something similar, are suitable.

Recording
Record the results on a testing chart as shown.

Boat	No of cargo pieces
A	4 Lego pieces
B	1 Lego piece
C	8 Lego pieces

Follow-up 2
Repeat the experiment with boats made of aluminium foil. Do these float better?

Submarines

Age range
Seven to nine.

Group size
Pairs or small groups.

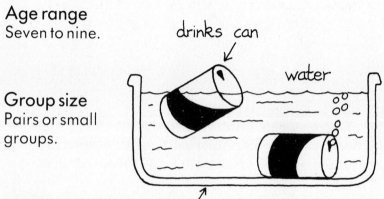

What you need
Soft drink cans, drinking straws, washing-up bowl, basin, or water-trough, water.

What to do
Give the children two soft drink cans, one full of air and one full of water. Let them feel the weight of each. Is the empty can really empty? What happens when the two cans are put into a basin of water? Ask them to try pushing down on the empty can and see what happens. Then try holding it under the surface of the water; what do they see? Bubbles of air will rise until the can eventually sinks.
Beware of the sharp holes on some cans.

Follow-up
Can the children find a way to make the can float to the surface again without touching it? (Try inserting a straw and blowing air back into the can.) Explain that submarines work on this principle.

Water pressure

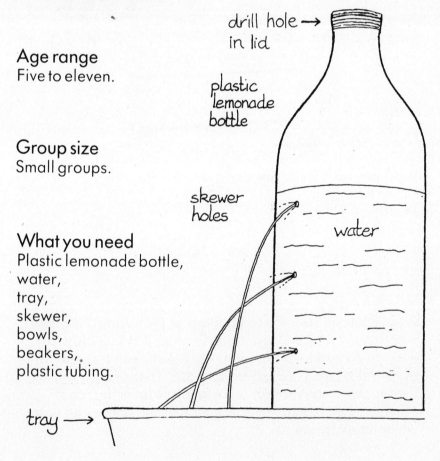

Age range
Five to eleven.

Group size
Small groups.

What you need
Plastic lemonade bottle, water, tray, skewer, bowls, beakers, plastic tubing.

What to do

The teacher can make small holes with a skewer at regular intervals in a plastic lemonade bottle. Stand the bottle in a tray or basin and watch the water spurt out through the holes. What happens? Ask the children from which hole the water is shooting furthest. Does the distance it travels change? If so, when does it go furthest?

Recording

Draw the paths taken by the water. Older children can measure and record how far each hole projects the water.

Follow-up

Do older children know what a siphon is? Try to explain. See if they can make a siphon using two beakers and a length of plastic tubing. Arrange them as in the diagram, ensuring that the water level in beaker A is higher than the end of the tube in beaker B. Suck water from beaker A into the tube until it is full. Place a finger over the free end of the tube, and place it in beaker B below the water level. Remove your finger and the water will flow from A to B. Raise and lower each beaker in turn. What happens?

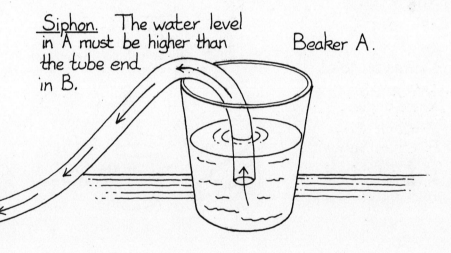

Siphon. The water level in A must be higher than the tube end in B.

Beaker A.

Beaker B

plastic tubing

Does this affect the direction of water flow? Can the children think of a way of stopping the water flow, without simply blocking it with a thumb?

Do the children know of any examples where this effect is used? Do they know where the water tank is installed at home?

Squirt power

Age range
Five to eleven.

Group size
Whole class.

What you need
Empty washing-up
liquid bottle,
bicycle pump,
plastic syringe,
water pistol,
water,
buckets and basins.

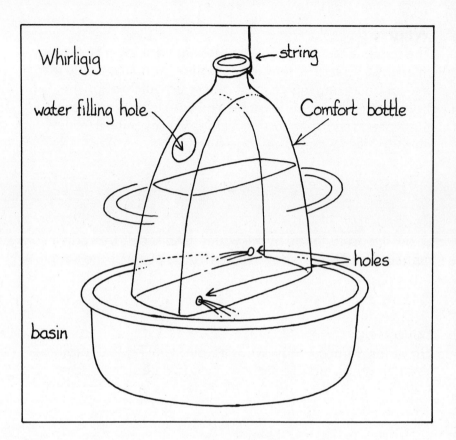

What to do
If children have played with water pistols, they should
know that if water is put under pressure it moves quickly
and forcefully. A number of activities demonstrate this;
they are mostly fairly messy, suitable for the playground in
summer and requiring careful class control. But they are
fun! How far can the class manage to squirt water from an
old washing-up liquid bottle over a measured distance?

What about from a water pistol, a bicycle pump, or a
plastic syringe?

Can they use the power of water pressure to drive
anything? Talk about water-wheels and water-mills. Try
building the whirligig shown here with a group of children:
you may have to do the cutting. Ask them to predict what
will happen and explain why. Test the model – with due
precaution! Do four holes give more power than two?

Boats

Age range
Five to eleven.

Group size
Small groups.

What you need
Water,
plastic guttering,
supermarket food trays,
balloons,
drinking straws,
newspaper,
hair drier,
elastic bands,
wood,
cane or dowelling,
hand drill and saw,
PVA glue,
plastic strip.

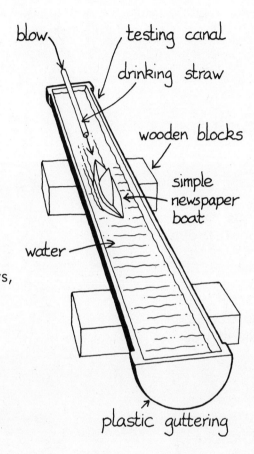

What to do
Set the children a challenge: to try to design a boat that will travel as far as possible without being pushed.

Infants can make a very simple boat out of newspaper and blow it along with a straw. Balloons are a good

source of power: various wind-powered models have already been shown on page 46. Hair driers provide a useful source of wind **(but beware, of course, of electrical appliances being used near water).** Elastic bands provide another means of propulsion. Older children able to use tools might come up with a boat like the one in the diagram.

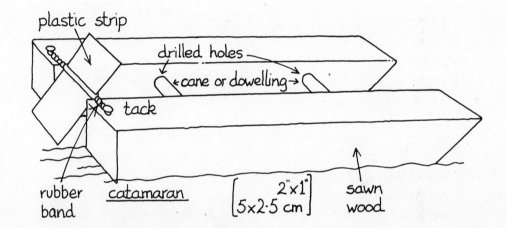

Recording
A good testing canal can be made from a length of raised plastic guttering filled with water. Measure the distances travelled and make comparisons. Record them on testing charts.

Follow-up
Can the children find ways of steering their boats? Test and record the results.

Water level

Age range
Five to nine.

Group size
Pairs.

What you need
Water,
glass jars,
marbles or washers,
elastic bands
or waterproof markers.

marbles

What to do
Ask the children to predict what will happen to the water level if they drop an object that sinks into a jar of water, then get them to do it. What does happen? Why do they think this is? Try adding objects to the water in a controlled series: washers on a string, or marbles of the same size dropped in one by one. The children can mark the level each time the water rises, with elastic bands around the jar, or with waterproof markers. What happens when the objects are systematically removed?

Solutions

Age range
Seven to eleven.

Group size
Small groups.

What you need
Glass jars,
water,
containers,
sand,
sugar,
salt,
soil,
flour,
teaspoon,
pencil,
Plasticine.

90

What to do

Begin by asking the children what happens to sugar when it's put into a cup of tea. Where do they think it goes? What happens to coffee powder in water? Let them try it out, see it dissolve and taste it. Let them find out that when a substance dissolves it spreads right through a liquid. Have available marked containers of different substances: sugar, salt, flour, sand, soil, etc. Ask the children what they think will happen to each of these when they are dropped in water. Test by putting a teaspoonful of each substance into a jar of water.

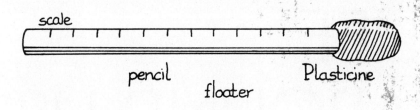

Follow-up

Make solutions of salt. Is there a limit to the amount of salt you can add to a small volume of water before no more will dissolve? Is there a difference in the way things float in salty and fresh water? Try floating objects in a very strong solution. Show the children a picture of people swimming in the Dead Sea.

Make a floater – a pencil scored at regular intervals, with a blob of Plasticine on the end. Try it in salty water and in tap water and note whereabouts on the scale the water level is each time. Try solutions of different strengths: 10 spoonfuls of salt; 20 spoonfuls of salt; 50 spoonfuls, etc.

substance	solubility
salt	✓
sand	✗
sugar	✓

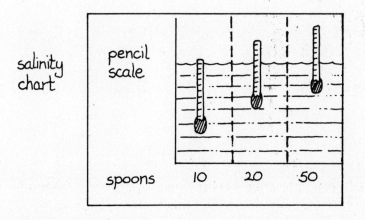

Recording

Record the results on a testing chart. Do all substances dissolve at the same rate? Can you make things dissolve faster? How?

Recording

The results could be recorded with a pictorial diagram as shown.

LIFE
AROUND US

Starter

Age range
Five to eleven.

Group size
Whole class.

What you need
Variety of seeds from packets, examples of as many seeds and fruits as possible, paper, pens.

What to do
The children make a collection of seeds, pips and stones: melon, apple, date, avocado pear, orange, lemon, oak, ash, sycamore, chestnut, pea, bean and so on. Discuss the seeds as you examine them with the children. How do they grow on the plant? How are they dispersed? Encourage the children to describe them as fully as possible.

Recording
The children can mount a display of seed samples together with descriptive labels.

Follow-up 1
If the school has a hamster or a guinea-pig, suggest that the children look at its food. Can they find any seeds? If they do, sow them and see what plants grow.

Make a collection of seeds and fruits from plants growing around the school. Children will probably find dandelion, willow herb, shepherd's purse, vetch, plantain and groundsel, to name a few. This will reinforce the association of fruits and seeds with flowering plants.

Recording
Using pictures from seed packets and catalogues, and the seeds themselves, children can draw a map to show which seeds produce which plant. Ask them to guess first.

Follow-up 2
Encourage the children to sort, group and classify the seeds. The criteria considered might include those with wings; those in hard cases; those in soft cases; seeds from trees; seeds from flowers; black seeds and white seeds; long, thin seeds and round, flat seeds.

Oranges and lemons

Age range
Five to nine.

Group size
Whole class.

What you need
Knife,
rulers,
hand lens,
oranges, lemons,
cucumbers, conkers,
tomatoes, peas,
apples, etc.

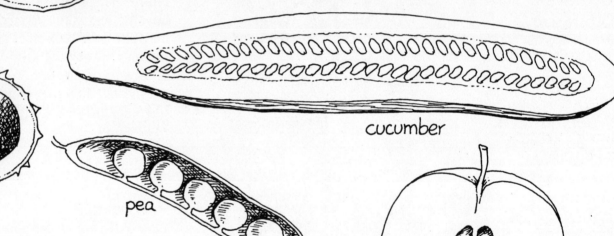

tomato

conker

pea

cucumber

apple

Recording
Ask them to draw their fruit as accurately as possible, pinpointing the seeds, flesh and outer skin. They should explain what they think each part is for, and estimate how many plants could be grown from this one fruit. Encourage them to draw large and colourful pictures.

What to do
The children collect a variety of common fruits. They should be cut in half, either horizontally or vertically. You should do this for the younger children; older children can do it for themselves. Examine the fruits carefully with a hand lens and measure them.

Follow-up
Children can swap their samples and compare fruit of the same kind and fruit of different kinds. Do the biggest fruits have the biggest seeds? Look at apples, cucumbers and peas. Does the smallest orange have the smallest pips? Do all apples have the same number of seeds?

94

Germination

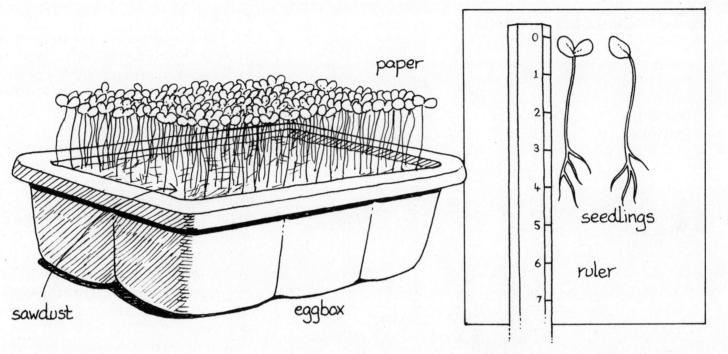

paper

sawdust

eggbox

seedlings

ruler

Age range
Seven to eleven.

Group size
Small groups.

What you need
Cress seeds,
egg boxes or
plastic cake trays,
polythene bags,
ruler,
sawdust, soil,
or cotton wool,
testing charts.

What to do
The children can grow cress seeds in different media.
Sawdust works well; cotton wool or soil can also be used.
Try growing them with water and without water, in the light
and in the dark. Try growing them in water only.

Egg boxes make good seed trays, as do empty plastic
trays from packets of biscuits or cakes. To prevent the
seed trays drying out over the weekend, slide them into
transparent polythene bags.

When the children examine the seeds to see which have
grown best, talk to them about what they mean by 'best'.
They may suggest height of seedlings, greenness,
sturdiness, speed of growth. They should consider roots as
well as shoots. Do the conditions which give the best
results for one kind of seed give the best results for other
kinds? Which growing medium is the most successful?

Recording
Use testing charts to record the results.

Roots and shoots

Age range
Five to nine.

Group size
Small groups.

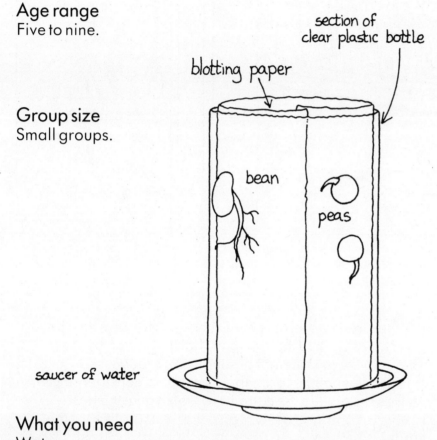

section of
clear plastic bottle

blotting paper

bean

peas

saucer of water

What you need
Water,
saucer,
blotting paper,
plastic lemonade bottles,
various seeds,
testing charts.

What to do
The teacher can cut out the middle straight-sided sections of clear plastic lemonade bottles. These can be lined with blotting paper and placed in a saucer of water. Different seeds can be placed between the blotting paper and the plastic, so that their shoots will show as they appear.

Runner beans are normally used for tests such as these. The children might care to try other seeds and compare them: peas, mung beans, black-eye beans, maize (popcorn) and sunflowers are alternatives. The experiment can be varied: try growing the seeds with and without water; in the light and in the dark; in different locations.

Do seeds grow better if they are soaked in water first? Do they grow better in a dark or a light place? Which emerges first from the seed — the root or the shoot? What happens to the seedcase when the root and shoot begin to show?

Do the root and shoot emerge from the same place in each seed? How quickly does each grow? Do their growth rates alter? Can you find a way of making a seed grow a much longer root? Encourage the children to ask their own questions, predict what will happen and explain their findings.

Recording
Record the results with testing charts.

Plant attractions

Age range
Seven to eleven.

Group size
Small groups.

What you need
Two sheets of perspex,
blotting paper,
tin lid,
two house bricks,
water,
sticky tape,
radish seeds.

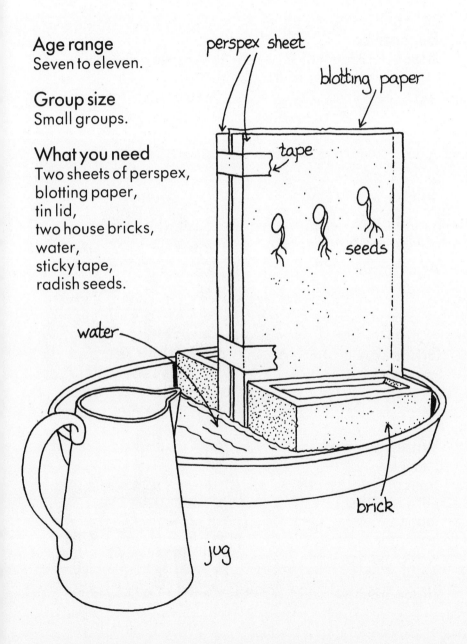

perspex sheet

blotting paper

tape

seeds

water

brick

jug

What to do
Another apparatus can easily be assembled in order to
display the way in which shoots develop. Seeds and
blotting paper are sandwiched between two sheets of
perspex held up by bricks in a tray of water – a large tin lid
would do. Make sure that the base of the blotting paper is
in the water and that the tray does not dry out.

Ask the children to watch the growth of radish seeds.
When the shoots are about two or three centimetres long,
invert the perspex so that the shoots are pointing
downwards. Ask the children to observe what happens
over the next few days, and try to explain why it happens.
Discuss the way in which shoots are attracted to light and
water; older children might look up the terms 'geotropism'
and 'phototropism' in the dictionary.

Recording
Each stage of the seeds' growth should be recorded in
drawings by the children.

Seed dispersal

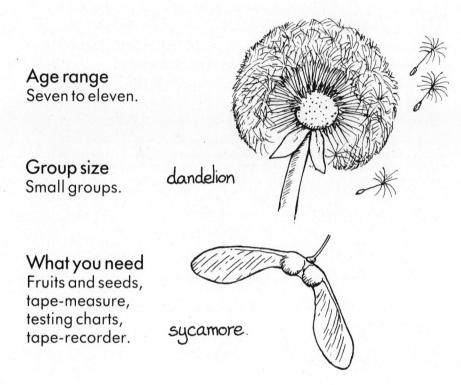

Age range
Seven to eleven.

Group size
Small groups.

What you need
Fruits and seeds, tape-measure, testing charts, tape-recorder.

dandelion

sycamore.

What to do
Let the children look at various plants and trees growing near the school and examine their fruits and seeds. How are the seeds dispersed? Are they hooked, like burs? Perhaps the fruit is eaten by a bird, and the seed spread in this way. Do the seeds float gently through the air like those of the dandelion? Or do the fruits spin and fly like those of the ash? Compare how fruits fly on still days and on windy days.

Search near trees for last year's seedlings. Measure the distance they have travelled. Why is this distance so important?

Recording
A tape-recorder could be used for an oral presentation of the activities carried out by the children.

Tree survey

Age range
Seven to eleven.

Group size
Small groups.

What you need
Leaves,
fruits,
nuts,
log,
bark,
wax crayons,
paper,
clipboards.

bark rubbing

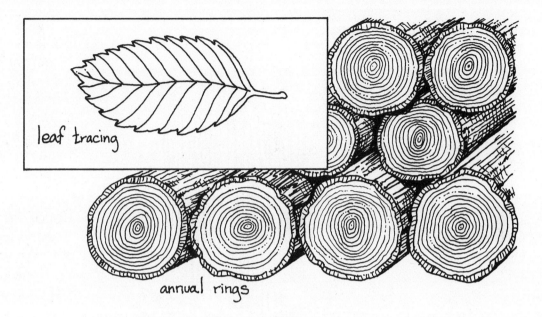

leaf tracing

annual rings

Children can draw the canopy shape; trace a leaf, showing the veins; make a bark rubbing, using a wax crayon or cobbler's wax.

What to do
Do you have any trees in your school playground? Or is there a park near your school? An interesting way to start a tree survey is to give each child in the group part of a tree: a leaf, a fruit, a flower, or whatever is available. Ask the children to look for that particular tree. When they have found it they should describe it as fully as possible, thinking about shape, texture, colour, etc.

Choose a tree. Talk about its various parts: the crown, the canopy, the branches, trunk and roots. Which way are the branches pointing? What shape is the tree? Where are the leaves, if any? Are they evergreen or deciduous? What does the bark look like; is it rough or smooth? Can you identify the tree?

Recording
On pages 123 and 124 you will find tree survey charts which can be photocopied. These provide an ideal way of recording what is found.

Follow-up
Collections of leaves, nuts and bark are useful for display and for discussion in the classroom. Let the children count the annual growth rings on a sawn log.

Measuring trees

Age range
Five to eleven.

Group size
Large group.

What you need
Skittles
or tent pegs,
string,
tape-measure,
squared paper,
scissors,
thermometer.

measuring girth

What to do
Can the children measure the girth of a tree by joining hands around the trunk? Young children might find it easier to do this by using string, cutting it to the circumference of the trunk. They can measure the girth at different heights. Can they find the diameter of the trunk? How?

The area of the canopy is rather harder to measure. One person should stand at some distance from the tree and direct another until he or she appears to be directly under the outside edge of the canopy. That spot is then marked with a tent peg or a skittle. The process is repeated from different angles until the whole area has been marked out. The distance from the trunk to each peg can be measured (with younger children, in paces).

Recording
The canopy shape can be plotted on graph paper, with, say, one square per one metre or pace. The angles from the trunk to the various markers will have to be estimated, so the result will only be approximate.

staking out the canopy area.

Follow-up
Is there a difference in the ground covering under the canopy? Are there more things growing, or less? Is there a difference in the air or ground temperature between the open field and the canopy area?

Leaf study

Age range
Seven to eleven.

Group size
Pairs or small groups.

What you need
Leaves,
graph paper,
balance,
hand lens,
plaster of Paris.

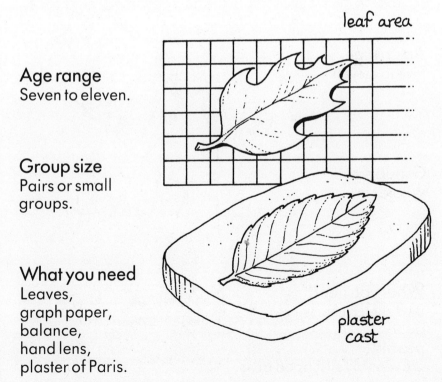
leaf area

plaster cast

What to do
The children choose one tree for a leaf study. Suggest that they look for the largest leaf they can find. They then measure the width and the length. By tracing the outline of the leaf on to squared paper they can find out its area. Remember, over half a square counts as one, under half as none.

Can they find the weight of one leaf? To do this they may need to weigh ten or even 50 leaves together and then divide the result by the total number of leaves. It may be best to use a straw balance. One group can estimate the number of leaves on one tree, and then estimate the weight of leaves on it.

Follow-up
The children should carry out a detailed examination of different leaves. Look at colour and shades of colour, texture, the way in which the veins branch and the edges of the leaves. They should use a hand lens. How many leaves are there on one twig? How are they grouped? Where are the biggest leaves on the twig?

Recording
Leaves can be pressed, dried and mounted for a display. You might try making plaster casts of different species.

Tree census

Age range
Seven to eleven.

Group size
Whole class.

What you need
Tree identification chart,
squared paper,
pencils,
crayons.

tree	1	2	3	4
oak				
ash				
plane				
beech				
holly				
birch				
larch				

census graph

What to do
Choose an area of woodland or park. Are most of the
trees conifers or broadleaved? Which is the most common
kind? The children can refer to a suitable tree
information chart (see pages 123 and 124
reproducing? Look for saplings. Are they growing near
other trees? If so, do these affect their shape? What else
determines their shape: light, or wind direction? Are other
plants such as lichens or fungus growing on the trunk? Do
the lichens tend to grow on one side of the trunk? Why?

Recording
The children can prepare a simple graph of the tree
population within the chosen area.

Introducing birds

Age range
Five to eleven.

Group size
Whole class.

What you need
Bird sketch charts,
paper,
pencils,
crayons or felt-tipped pens.

chart on page 126 should provide the children with a valuable aid. When they have sketched in the outlines, they can add details of colour in the appropriate places.

The children should compare the sizes of birds. Are they larger or smaller than other birds with which they are familiar? They can then try grouping together birds with similar characteristics. What words are used to describe birds?

Recording
Display the bird drawings and the descriptions.

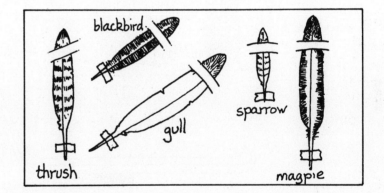

What to do
When beginning to study birds it is important to talk about their different shapes. By looking at their standing and flying or floating positions, and the shapes of their beaks, feet, wings and tails, children can learn to identify birds and at the same time learn why they look as they do. It is useful to find a simple way of drawing them, and the

Follow-up
Can the children find any feathers in the park or on the way to school? Try to identify them. Examine their structure under a hand lens. Make a feather display by taping the quills to paper or threading them through slits in the paper. Warn the children that birds tend to have fleas!

Bird-tables

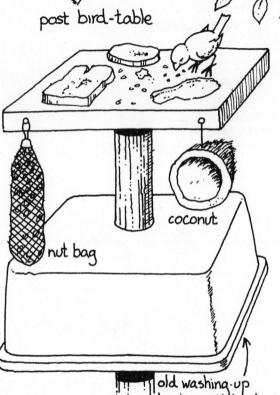

post bird-table

nut bag

coconut

old washing-up basin against cats

Age range
Five to eleven.

Group size
Small group or whole class.

What you need
Wood,
saw,
hammer,
nails,
food containers,
string,
tray,
bin lid.

What to do
The easiest time to watch birds is when they are feeding. Make a bird-table and set it up in the school grounds, where it can be observed from a window. Try and design one and site it with the children's help. It will need to be cat-proof. A hanging tray is one solution to the problem of cats, or fitting an inverted plastic basin around the post.

Do all the birds eat the same food? Ask the children to investigate. They may wish to concentrate on only one kind of bird, and make observations at different times during the day.

Put food on the table in separate containers: brown bread, fruit, seeds, nuts, bacon rind, cheese rind, etc. Which food is the most popular? Which birds eat it?

Look at feeding positions, whether the bird takes the food away with it, whether it chases other birds off the table or is chased away itself.

Another good time to watch birds is when they are drinking and bathing. Make a bird-bath with an upturned plastic bin lid supported by stones.

bird bath   bin lid

Recording
The children can use the chart on page 125 to record feeding and movement patterns.

Bird movements

Age range
Seven to eleven.

Group size
Small group or
whole class.

What you need
Pencils,
clipboards,
testing charts.

What to do
Ask the children to observe carefully how birds move. Do they all move in the same way? Watch them walking; does the bird hop with both feet together or take one step at a time? Do any birds do both? Watch the head and tail. Does the bird make any special movements with either of these parts?

Look at the way birds use their feet for standing and holding on to things. What can birds land on? Fences? Twigs? Water? Do they land with feet outstretched or straight down?

Take a look at flying. Where are the bird's legs and feet when it is in the air? Do all birds fly in the same way? Record their flight paths by drawing lines to show the patterns. Do they have fast or slow wing-beats?

How does the bird clean its feathers? What are birds doing when they preen themselves? Do they use anything other than water to bathe in?

Can the children explain how a bird's shape might affect the way it moves?

Recording
The movements of each bird can be recorded on the chart on page 125.

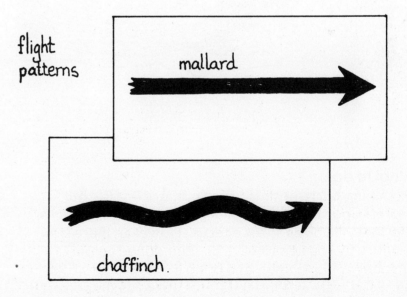

flight
patterns

mallard

chaffinch

Bird's nest

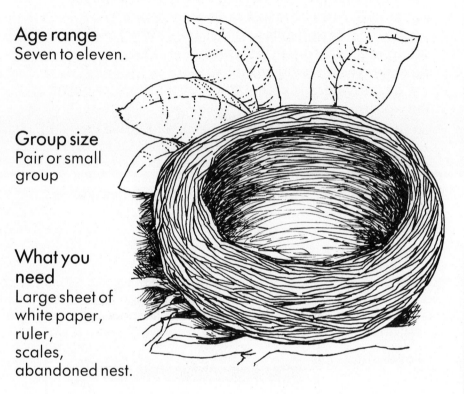

Age range
Seven to eleven.

Group size
Pair or small group

What you need
Large sheet of white paper, ruler, scales, abandoned nest.

What to do
Examining birds' nests is a fascinating exercise, but impress upon the children that they must *never* collect or interfere with birds' nests or eggs. However, there is no reason why you cannot take an abandoned nest in October or November, and bring it into the class. Examine the nest closely with the children. Look at its shape, and its inner and outer construction.

Recording
Ask them to draw the nest as accurately as possible. Measure its dimensions and weight, and record the results.

Follow-up
A group can unravel the nest on large sheets of paper and record the materials used in its construction. Is the inside made from different materials from the outside? What holds it together? In the spring and summer you can observe a nest in use, from a distance.

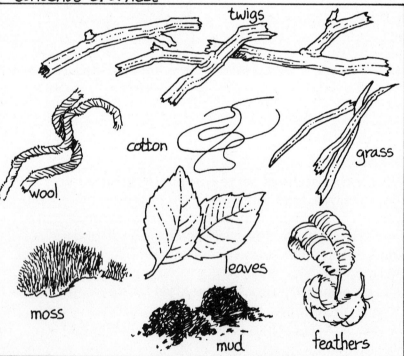

contents of a nest

twigs

cotton

grass

wool

leaves

moss

mud

feathers

Minibeast search

Age range
Five to nine.

Group size
Small group or whole class.

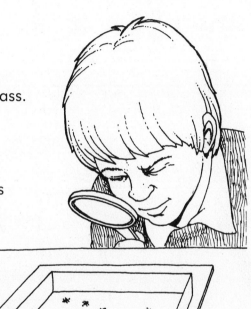

What you need
Transparent plastic pots
and nylon,
or Petri dishes,
elastic bands,
paintbrushes,
hand lenses,
paper,
papier mâché,
wire,
testing charts.

What to do
Discuss with the children what we mean by a minibeast – a small creature without a backbone, such as a spider, an insect or a woodlouse. Have a preliminary look and then ask the children to explore the playground or field and search for minibeasts. Discuss likely places to search –
under stones, under logs or polythene sheeting, in trees and on bark, among roots and fallen leaves.

Talk about methods of collecting the creatures for observation. What can the children suggest? Transparent plastic dessert pots with nylon tops secured by elastic bands are useful with younger children. Paintbrushes can be used to transfer creatures into the containers. Remind children to be very careful if Petri dishes are being used. Hand lenses are very useful; tie them around the children's necks to avoid breakages. All creatures should be returned once they have been examined.

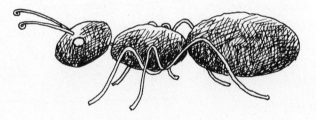

Recording
The children should observe the creatures carefully, recording all the details with the help of the chart on page 122. Discuss the findings. The children can draw their minibeasts in colour, or even make models using wire and papier mâché. If there are enough children, a census of the playground's minibeast population can be carried out.

Minibeast experiments

Age range
Seven to nine.

Group size
Small groups.

What you need
Plastic tray,
soil,
cardboard box,
woodlice,
foodstuffs,
water.

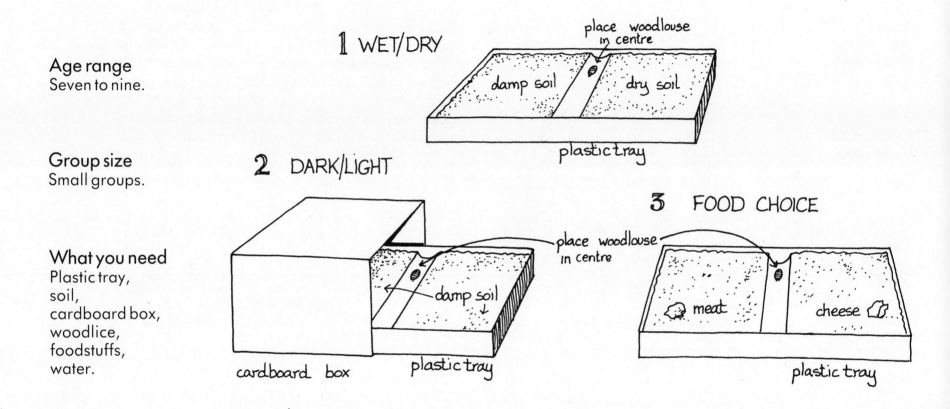

What to do
Set the children a challenge: can they devise a way of discovering the conditions in which woodlice prefer to live? A solution is to set up a plastic tray, half of which is covered in dry soil, and half of which is covered in damp soil. The woodlouse can be placed in the centre. Which side does it choose most often?

Use similar tests, varying one element at a time, to investigate the preferred light conditions – shaded or open – and foodstuffs. Try different foods: leaves, meat, fruit, etc. Why do the children think a particular food is chosen?

Recording
Use a chart to record the results of the tests, and let the children discuss their findings.

Minibeast traps

1 Pitfall trap

stick　　slate　　stick

glass jar

← hole in ground

suitable food

2 Pooter

1ˢᵗ tube

2ⁿᵈ tube

sealed jam jar

end covered in tissue secured by elastic band

Age range
Seven to eleven.

Group size
Small groups.

What you need
Glass jars,
piece of slate
or tile,
bait,
plastic tubing,
tissue,
rubber band.

What to do
Once the children have discovered the conditions that minibeasts prefer, can they design and set up their own traps? Two traps which should bring in a good catch are the pitfall trap and the pooter, both shown on this page. **It is essential that you check the children's designs and impress on them that they should never trap living creatures except under adult supervision.**

Recording
Identify the minibeasts trapped and record the results on charts. Release the animals in their original habitat.

Pond dipping

⊗

Age range
Seven to eleven.

Group size
Small group or whole class.

What you need
Bamboo,
nylon tights,
coat-hanger wire,
string,
glass jars,
polythene bags,
shallow
white dishes,
hand lenses,
paper,
pencil,
clipboards,
plastic bucket.

What to do
The best time for pond dipping is probably between April and October. During this period even a small ditch will be teeming with life.

Pond dipping requires very careful supervision of children. They should wear boots and appropriate clothing: beware of broken bottles and rusty iron. Ensure that the habitat is disturbed as little as possible. All creatures collected for examination *must* be returned to the water.

Collecting gear can be made by the children: the diagrams on the opposite page are examples.

Before you start, ask the children to look at the pond's surroundings. Is it in a sheltered or an open spot? What is the water like? Is it clean or murky? Stagnant or moving?

When dipping, the children should sweep their nets through the water without stirring up the mud. Turn the nets inside out into shallow dishes of pond water. They can also make a surface skim; search weed for eggs, snails, etc, and lift stones and wood.

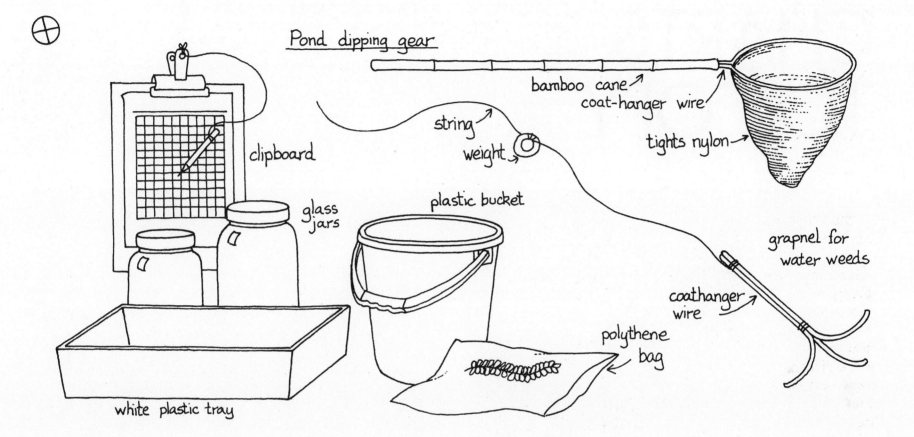

Pond dipping gear

clipboard

glass jars

white plastic tray

string

weight

plastic bucket

polythene bag

bamboo cane

coat-hanger wire

tights nylon

grapnel for water weeds

coathanger wire

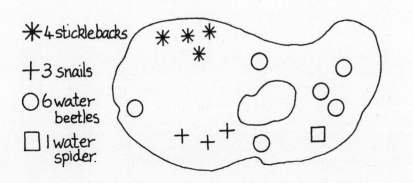

✳ 4 sticklebacks

+ 3 snails

○ 6 water beetles

□ 1 water spider.

Recording
Ask the children to make careful drawings of what they see, using hand lenses for greater detail. Estimate the size of each creature. How many creatures can be found? Do different creatures live in different parts of the pond? How does each one move?

CHARTS
TO COPY

Testing chart

Name:

Class:

Subject:

Testing chart							

Name: **Class:**

Subject:

1-cm squares

Name:

Class:

2-cm squares

Name: Class:

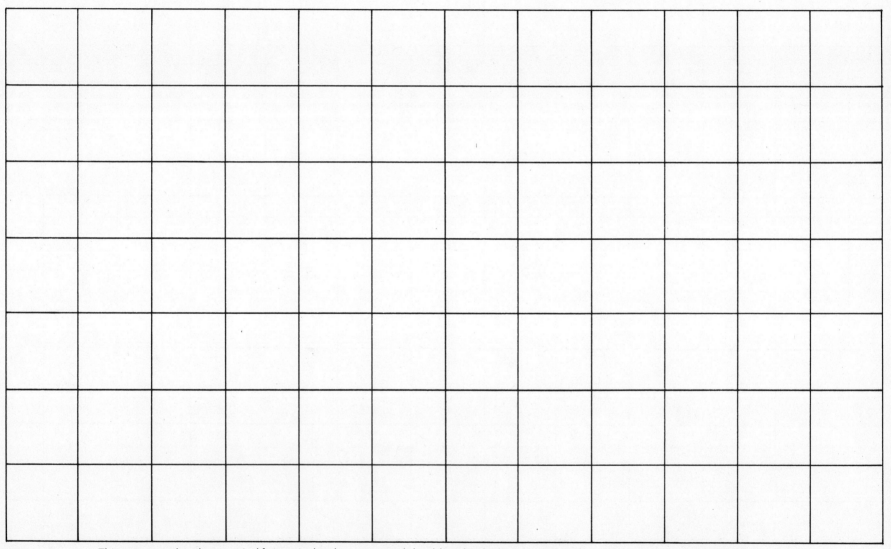

This page may be photocopied for use in the classroom and should not be declared in any return in respect of any photocopying licence.

5-cm squares

Name: Class:

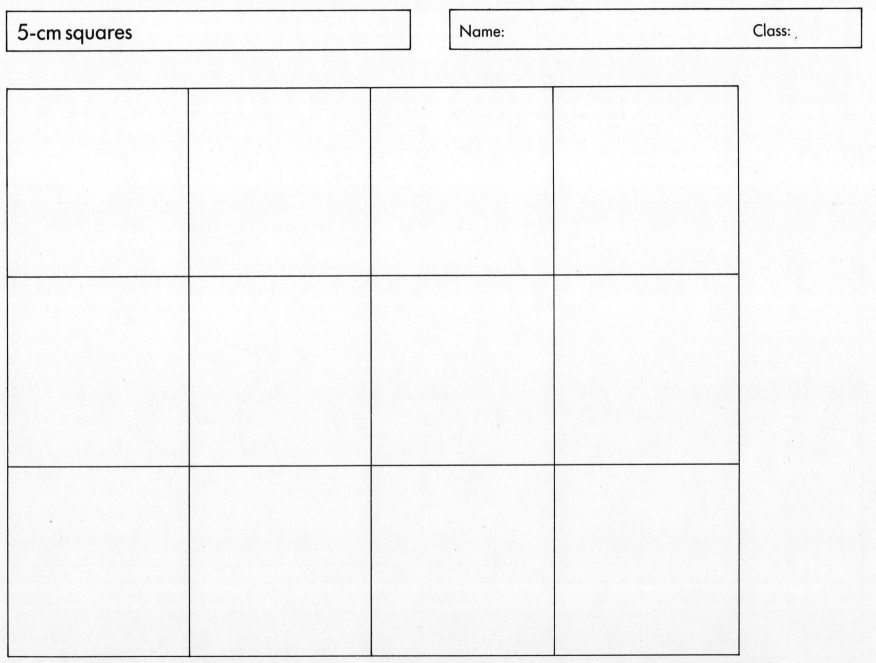

Graph chart	Name:	Class:

Subject:

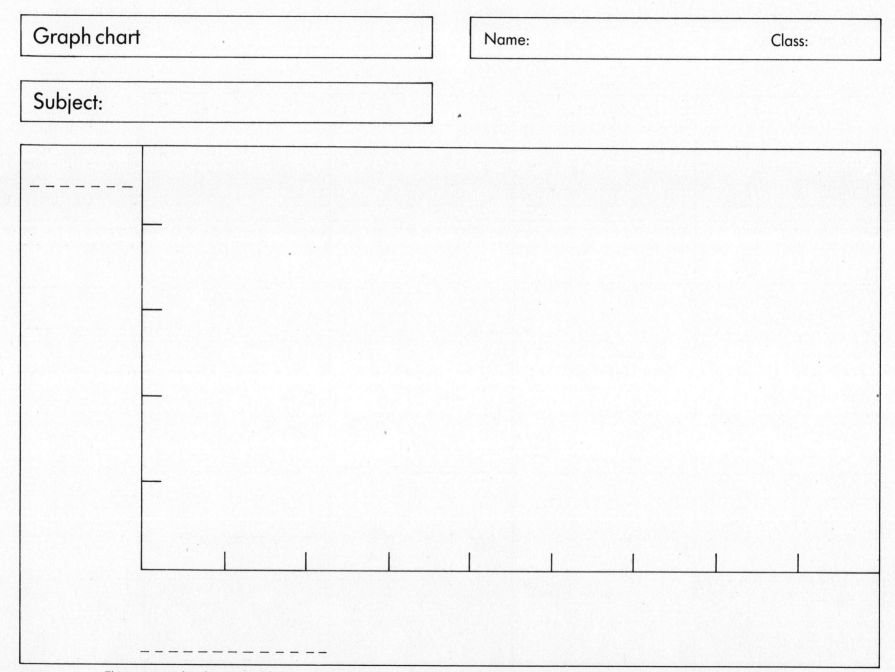

This page may be photocopied for use in the classroom and should not be declared in any return in respect of any photocopying licence.

Body chart		Name:			Class:	
	Beginning term 1	End term 1	Beginning term 2	End term 2	Beginning term 3	End term 3
Height						
Waist						
Chest						
Leg length						
Arm length						
Arm span						
Hand area						
Hand span						
Foot area						
Foot length						
Weight						
Hair colour						
Eye colour						

Fingerprint chart	Name:	Class:
	Sex:	Age:

Remember: roll the finger from side to side to get a good print.

Whorl   Loop   Arch   Composite.

Left hand: write in print type

Little finger _____

Third finger _____

Second finger _____

Index finger _____

Thumb _____

Right hand: write in print type

Little finger _____

Third finger _____

Second finger _____

Index finger _____

Thumb _____

Weekly weather chart					Name:				Class:			

Week	Date	Rainfall	Wind force			Wind direction (N, NE, E, SE, S, SW, W, NW)			Temperature – °C ground level			Temperature – °C one metre in air		
day			am	noon	pm	am	noon	pm	am	noon	pm	am	noon	pm
Monday														
Tuesday														
Wednesday														
Thursday														
Friday														

| Minibeast chart | | | | Name: | Class: |

Minibeast chart

Kind of minibeast spotted

Place spotted

Is the body in segments?	Yes/no	How many?	

Does it have legs?	Yes/no	How many?	

How are the legs arranged?	Separated?	Close together?
Tick here		

Does it have wings?	Yes/no	How many?	Tick box
Have the wings many veins or few?		One pair	
		Two pairs	
Describe the texture of the wings		Two pairs (one hidden)	

Does the creature have a shell?	Yes/no
Is the body hairy or smooth?	Hairy/smooth

Name: **Class:**

Draw a large picture of the creature here

Draw details of head here	Draw details of leg here

Is the head longer than it is wide?	Yes/no
Does the creature have a shell?	Yes/no

Tree information chart 1

Name:	Class:

Make a map and mark the position of your tree

Tree girth	at ground level	at one metre up

Use some words to describe your tree

Draw the canopy shape here

Leaf colour chart: mix paints to match leaf

January	February	March	April
May	June	July	August
September	October	November	December

Estimated area of canopy

| Tree information chart 2 | Name: | Class: |

Draw any seed, flower or fruit

Draw anything living on your tree

Draw your leaf here — count its area in cm square Area:

Bird feeding and movement chart

Name: **Class:**

Place observed

Date   **Time**

Species (guess)

Alone or in a group?

Main colour	Other colours

Does it	walk?	or hop?
Tick here		

Beak shape				
Tick here				

Tail shape				
Tick here				

Body position			
Tick here			

Draw flight pattern:

Does it land to eat?	Yes/no

Does it chase away other birds?	Yes/no

Types of food eaten

Bird sketch chart

Name: Class:

For birds with sloping bodies,
like robins, thrushes, crows.

For birds with horizontal bodies,
like mallard, moorhen.

For birds with upright bodies,
like owls, guillemots.

For birds with long necks and
horizontal bodies, like geese, swans.

Books to read

All About Me (5–8), Trefor Williams (Nelson, 19).

Air and Water Activities, Dorothy Diamond (Hulton, 1984).

Practical Primary Science, Romola Showell (Ward Lock Educational, 1983).

Read and Do series, Doug Kincaid and Peter Coles (Arnold Wheaton, various dates). *Hot and Cold, Light and Dark, Quiet and Loud, Wet and Dry, Touch and Feel, Ears and Hearing, Taste and Smell, Eyes and Looking.*

Science in Primary Education (ASE) *Paper No 2 Role of the Head, Paper No 3 Role of the Post-holder.*

Science 5/13 series, sponsored by the Schools' Council, The Nuffield Foundation and the Scottish Education Council (Macdonald Educational, various dates). *Early Experiences, Early Explorations, Investigations 1 and 2, Tackling Problems 1 and 2, Ways and Means, Working With Wood 1 and 2 and Background Information, Time 1 and 2 and Background, Science from Toys 1 and 2 and Background, Structures and Forces 1 and 2, Holes, Gaps and Cavities 1 and 2, Minibeasts 1 and 2, Change 1 and 2 and Background, Metals 1 and 2 and Background, Ourselves 1 and 2, Like and Unlike 1 and 2, Trees 1 and 2, Coloured Things 1 and 2, Children and Plastics 1 and 2 and Background.*

Science in a Topic series, Doug Kincaid and Peter Coles (Hulton, various dates) *Food, Clothes and Costume, Sports and Games.*

Starting Primary Science, Megan Hayes (Edward Arnold, 1982).

Teaching Primary Science series, a Chelsea College Project sponsored by the Nuffield Foundation and the Social Science Research Council (Macdonald Educational, various dates) *Candles, Seeds and Seedlings, Paints and Materials, Science from Waterplay, Fibres and Fabrics, Mirrors and Magnifiers, Science from Wood, Musical Instruments, Aerial Models, Teachers' Guide to Primary Science.*

The Clue Books series, G Allen and J Denslow (Oxford University Press, various dates) *Trees, Insects, Birds.*

Think Well (9–13), Trefor Williams *et al* (Nelson, 1977).

Equipment suppliers

E J Arnold,
Butterley Street,
Leeds LS10 1AX,
Yorkshire.

Griffin & George Ltd,
285 Ealing Road,
Alperton,
Wembley,
Middlesex.

Hestair Hope Ltd,
St Philip's Drive,
Royton,
Oldham OL2 6AG,
Lancashire.

Osmiroid Educational,
E S Perry Ltd,
Osmiroid Works,
Gosport,
Hampshire.

Philip Harris Ltd,
Lynn Lane,
Shenstone,
Staffordshire.

A great deal of material can be obtained locally from Woolworths and similar stores, warehouses, clearance stores, or local authority suppliers. Try factories for wood, paper, plastics, fabrics and mirror offcuts.

Measuring and recording materials

rulers
pencils
felt-tipped pens
clipboards
graph paper
plain paper
lined paper
blotting paper
glue
Plasticine
Blu-Tack
timers
scales
tape-measures
scissors
measuring jugs
thermometers
spring balances

Collections of scrap materials

papers
fabrics
wood
stones
elastic bands
glues
tubes
plastic containers
yoghurt pots
washing-up liquid bottles
jam-jars

strings and threads
polystyrene
balloons
polythene bags
drinking straws
candles
nuts, nails, screws
shells

Scientific equipment

mirrors
lenses
nets
magnets
batteries
bulbs
a vast selection of containers
torches
heat source equipment
selection of bowls
magnifiers
tweezers
tools
pliers
junior hacksaw
drill and bits
hammer
screwdrivers
vice/clamp
plumb-line
knives, forks, spoons
bicycle pump
oven
gardening tools